SUBLIMINAL
SELLING
SKILLS

SUBLIMINAL SELLING SKILLS

KERRY L. JOHNSON

amacom

AMERICAN MANAGEMENT ASSOCIATION

This book is available at a special
discount when ordered in bulk quantities.
For information, contact Special Sales Department,
AMACOM, a division of American Management Association,
135 West 50th Street, New York, NY 10020.

Library of Congress Cataloging-in-Publication

Johnson, Kerry L.
    Subliminal selling skills.

    Bibliography: p.
    Includes index.
    1. Selling—Psychological aspects.   2. Consumer
behavior.   I. Title.
    HF5438.8.P75J65   1988   658.8'5'019   88-47694
    ISBN 0-8144-7708-9

Printing number

10 9 8 7 6 5 4 3 2 1

To my kids,
Stacey and Neil,
may God bless you always.

Contents

Preface

You have entered into the world of subliminal selling skills. From this book, you will learn some of the most sophisticated, yet easy-to-use, sales psychology techniques ever discovered.

Over the last decade, I have studied why it is that master communicators and sales superstars can literally cause us to gravitate towards them. I have also discovered why it is that some people with a few gestures or words can communicate mountains of knowledge and information and, more importantly, evoke emotion to such an extent that their listeners become committed and dedicated to what these communicators say.

The result of my research is *Subliminal Selling Skills*, which shows you how subliminal selling works and how you can apply the techniques used by sales superstars in your own selling or interpersonal communication. Just as advertisers can persuade people to buy without the consumer really knowing why or how, so can you.

You'll learn how the unconscious mind works and how you can directly appeal and present information to the unconscious in the most persuasive way possible. You'll also learn how to effectively bypass objections when communicating your ideas. And you'll discover some fundamentally simple ways to effectively communicate with absolutely everyone.

A quick word on the structure of this book. It is informally divided into three parts. The first part, consisting of Chapters 1 through 4, explores the workings of neuro-linguistic programming, a term coined by Bandler and Grinder and discussed in Chapter 1. This technique will help you determine how your clients think and how best to approach them. The second part, Chapters 5 through 15, features a variety of techniques that you can use to build rapport with your prospects and clients. Many of the topics covered in these chapters will be familiar to you. What I have done here is to dissect each technique so that you can understand its psychological underpinnings. Occasionally, the detailed discussions may appear simplistic, but bear with them. Altogether, these techniques will equip you with a hands-on understanding of subliminal selling skills. The third part gives you clues on closing, helping you to recognize when your client or prospect is ready to buy (Chapter 16), and brings all of the subliminal selling skills together (Chapter 17), showing you how to use neuro-linguistic programming, rapport-building techniques, and buying signals to sell your prospects.

A Glossary is featured at the end of the book. Here, you will find brief definitions for all of the major terms and concepts mentioned in the book.

Whenever possible, I have tried to avoid using sexist language. Occasionally, however, I use the pronoun "he" to refer to both men and women. The alternative choice would have been to use confusing sentence structure that would have made the book more difficult to read.

The names mentioned as examples in the text, while based on actual salespeople, are fictitious.

The bulk of the research for this book results from my years of field work as a consultant to salespeople in various professions.

Where appropriate I have cited outside sources of material, which can also be found in the section entitled Suggested Reading.

Personality Pattern Development: Nature or Nurture?

Have you ever wondered why some clients buy from you with very little information while others take an inordinate amount of time to make a decision? The psychological reason for such a discrepancy may lie in childhood development.

Jean Piaget, the Swiss psychologist who pioneered work in childhood development studies, determined that the bulk of our personality patterns are developed between ages 2 and 7. Who we are today and what we will be in the future largely depend on what happened to us during our early years.

One of the reasons why it is so difficult to change as human beings (e.g., to stop smoking, lose weight, or even change the ways we communicate) is that we act out our adult lives as an extension of what we experienced during childhood.

This childhood developmental period coupled with thought processes that we were born with determines the needs, desires, and motivations we now possess.

We all develop differently, and each of us has different behavior patterns. Beware of sales trainers who stand in front of you at sales conferences boasting that they have a surefire closing technique that will work *for everyone.* It's unlikely. If all prospects are not the same, how could one closing technique possibly work for every prospect or client?

In the early 1900s, prior to Piaget's groundbreaking work with child development theories, Sigmund Freud, the father of psychoanalysis, also surmised that adult behavior patterns were based on childhood experiences.

Another psychological researcher, B. F. Skinner, the leading proponent of the *behavioral* school of psychology, concluded that we are a product of the environmental stimuli we experience. Rewards and punishment influence our behavior. We tend to repeat those behaviors for which we are rewarded, while avoiding those that cause punishment.

Still other psychological and sociological theorists believe that our behavior is *predetermined.* They hold that we primarily act the way we do because of heredity.

The argument about whether our behavior is caused by biological or natural influences or from reactions to our environment and our nurturing has been an ongoing one for years. It is now referred to as the *nature vs. nurture argument.*

An argument can be made for the nature/biology/heredity explanation of behavior if we consider that studies have shown that identical twins separated at birth often display similar behavioral characteristics.

But studies in behavioral modification techniques suggest that by issuing rewards for desired behaviors and issuing punishment for undesirable forms of behavior, people do have the ability to change others in spite of hereditary influences.

What is more likely than nature or nurture being the sole reason for our behavior is that our behavior results from a mixture of the two. Our genes *and* our experiences combine to make us act as we do. While we all exhibit many behavioral characteristics, we often favor certain traits over others in our daily lives.

By understanding how people have come to behave the way they do, we can begin to understand how to meet their needs in a way that is acceptable to them.

Visuals, Auditories, and Kinesthetics

In this book, you will learn that people fall into three basic categories of behavioral modes. You'll learn about people Bandler and Grinder refer to as *visuals*, how to identify them and understand what they are like. You will learn what is going on in their minds and discover effective techniques to successfully sell to people who think in a visual mode.

You will learn about another group of people termed *auditories.* You will find out how to spot them and their characteristic mannerisms. You will discover their predominant mode of thinking and the best possible way to communicate with them to make sure that you will close your sale.

Kinesthetics, or feeling-based people, are the third group of people examined in this book. By learning how these people think, what they are like, and how they behave as well as how to persuade, sell, and communicate with them, you will have a good chance of getting them to act and react in a way you'd like.

While each of us may have some visual, auditory, and kinesthetic characteristics, we operate primarily out of one of these three different behavioral modes. Imagine the stellar results you will experience when you attempt to sell to people after identifying the mode in which they operate and can relate to them in language or actions they can best understand.

Building Better Rapport

You can't expect to be an effective salesperson without establishing trust and rapport with your prospects. I will show you techniques that will help you establish rapport within minutes of meeting with your customer. These techniques are surprisingly simple. They are called matching and mirroring.

I will also share with you some specific persuasion techniques to use when talking to your prospect on the telephone. You can actually change someone's attitude just by using subliminal messages.

I will show you how to *anchor* people's emotions and sell using your prospect's own nonverbal cues.

I will explore the strategy of *psychological sliding,* a sophisticated technique that allows you to disarm objections by moving your prospect's thought process from recognizing objections to seeing benefits.

With a technique called the *instant replay,* you will discover your prospect's unique decision-making or buying strategy. You will be able to understand exactly how your prospect will buy in just a few minutes. In turn, you'll be able to present your product or service to him in the way he wants to buy it.

You will find out how to use stories and metaphors—both effective sales tools—in just the way your prospect wants to hear them.

Finally, you will learn how to discover your prospect's needs and desires, how to probe and communicate with him like a pro, and how to fend off objections to your sales presentations.

Most important of all, you will see that you can wrap all of these techniques together to make a bundle of money by communicating with people the way they want to be communicated with—instead of the way you want to communicate with them.

When you've finished reading *Subliminal Selling Skills* and followed the advice presented, be prepared to sell more in the ensuing few weeks and months than you have ever sold in your whole life.

To remember these ideas:

1. Practice at least one technique a day in a real-life situation.
2. Teach the technique to two other people. That will solidify the ideas in your mind and help you find more applications for these concepts.

In the information that follows, you will be getting some of the most useful and effective psychological sales techniques available today. Let's begin now to uncover your subliminal selling skills!

Kerry L. Johnson, Ph.D.
Tustin, California
March 1988

Acknowledgments

This is my second book with Jeffrey L. Seglin as collaborator. He did a first-rate job in taking very sophisticated material and applying it to a very readable format. Thanks also to Ron Mallis, who realized that sales consists of more than closing techniques. This forward-thinking editor understood that sales relationships are based on trust, not on products. Thanks also to Evan Marshall, who not only has been a great adviser, but also has become a good friend. Thanks to my wife, Sandy, who has allowed me to travel four days a week to speak around the world in an effort to test my ideas.

SUBLIMINAL SELLING SKILLS

INTRODUCTION

Communicating With Prospects to Give Them What *They* Want

You are being subliminally seduced almost every day. There are subliminal messages surrounding you that either change your attitudes or make you more receptive to the persuasive messages that people want you to remember.

Subliminally Seduced at Every Turn

Casino management in Las Vegas has known for years how to subliminally manipulate its clientele.

- It knows that lowering the lights has a hypnotic, trancelike effect that relaxes you into playing games longer.
- Casinos rarely feature clocks or windows because management doesn't want you to think about what time it is. Casinos want you to run out of money before you run out of time.
- You will almost never see a slot machine by itself in a casino. Instead, you'll be surrounded by groups of four, five, and six machines. Casinos

want you to hear the money coming down the chutes of the slot machines surrounding you. They want you to think, as you pull that arm down, "this thing is going to hit any second now; I can hear all the jackpots around me."

K-Mart, the national department store, is doing practically the same thing. It too has learned to lower the lights to hypnotic levels, as well as to flash blue lights around special sale areas.

But K-Mart has also learned how to put subliminal messages in the Muzak playing over store loudspeakers. Industrial psychology studies have concluded that Muzak can increase worker performance and decrease worker tension if used in the right way, at the appropriate time of day.

K-Mart has taken its use of Muzak a step further, however, imbedding subliminal messages in the recordings to stop shoplifting. Repeated inaudibly under the Muzak over and over and over again during all store hours, the message commands, "Please don't steal."

K-Mart has reported a decrease of over 30 percent in shoplifting in just the few months since it began to use these subliminal crime-stopping messages. It has even determined an increase in sales beyond expectations.

Subliminal advertisements in the print media flow forth in endless supply. One of the most subliminal of these that I've come across lately is a magazine advertisement run by Cadbury Schweppes, Inc., for its Mounds and Almond Joy candy bars. The advertisement introduces the viewer of the full-color layout to the sensuality of deep, dark, rich flowing chocolate. The caption reads, "Oooo. . . . Ahhh. . . . Mounds and Almond Joy. Ooo and ahh for yourself."

Not only is the copy especially effective, but the light hitting the chocolate highlights very smooth, sexy curves on the chocolate being poured. In fact, if you turn the advertisement upside down, you can see the outline of a nude woman with her knees pulled up to her chest.

Cadbury Schweppes has masterfully and subliminally gotten to the sensuous chocolate fetish almost all of us have.

Selling Subliminally, Not Manipulatively

This book is certainly not going to teach you how to manipulate your prospects subliminally. What it *will* do is show you sophisticated techniques for communicating with people subliminally to help them get what they want.

I define "subliminal selling skills" as those techniques that enable you to sell prospects your products and services without their thinking they're being sold. By using subliminal selling techniques, you will be able to identify and communicate in your prospects' thought modes so that they buy more quickly from you and also say yes to your sales offering nearly every time. By using subliminal selling skills to help you identify your prospects' buying patterns and filling their needs, your closing rate will reach nearly 100 percent, because you are helping your prospects buy what they want.

You've been sold things without really knowing exactly how for years. Advertisers know how to sell to you with the right method, at the right time, in the right place. They know how much money you carry in your wallet, how far you drive to work each day. They know how much you spend per store visit. That knowledge is then turned into sales strategies that you find irresistible.

Now, you can use a similar type of selling system for yourself. You can target your customers and appeal to them in a way that makes them respond best. Subliminal selling skills gives you a customized approach to customers whose buying patterns all differ.

Letting Your
Prospects Double
Your Business

Have you ever felt, when face to face with one of your prospects, as if you weren't quite getting through? Have you ever felt that your prospect, during a face-to-face interaction, or even during a closed-door presentation, didn't quite see, hear, and feel the same level of excitement about your product as you did? Is your closing rate not yet at 100 percent?

I can guess the answers to all three of those questions. And I bet, without having to read your mind, that you wouldn't mind changing the answers to those questions for the better.

I'd like to bring you these three benefits as you read this book:

1. The ability to find out more about your prospects in five minutes than you previously could in two weeks.
2. The ability to gain more trust from your prospects faster than you ever thought possible.
3. Probably the most important benefit of all, the ability to double your business this year by using subliminal selling techniques.

This book will help you understand what your prospect is thinking while he is thinking it.

Unconscious Competence:
Million-Dollar Sales Techniques

A lot of the information in this book has come from observing salespeople who have excelled in their fields—for example, one, a life insurance agent in Toledo, is shocked if a prospect doesn't buy his products. In fact, he says his closing rate is 100 percent. Another big hitter does over $1 million each year as a financial planner. A peak producer from Vancouver, British Columbia, is a phenomenal salesman. He makes over $100,000 a month selling his products. He is brilliant in his use of persuasion skills, and knows exactly how to say the right thing at the right time.

These people are all incredibly successful. But do you know what? They don't know why they're doing so much business; they have no idea why they do so well.

If you ask them they may say,

> Well, you've got to have a positive mental attitude.
> You've got to be a winner. You've got to know what you
> want in life.

These big hitters have spent about twenty years each to get where they are now. They all have learned what to do and what not to do with their prospects.

But they can't tell you *how* they're selling. They can tell you what they think they're doing; but frankly, they have no idea how they do it. They are blessed with what I call *unconscious competence*.

Studying these million-dollar salespeople reveals one particularly interesting characteristic: In every case, these very highly productive salespeople *sell exactly the way their prospects want to buy.* Those salespeople I studied who are making substantially less than $1 million a year seem to sell as though they were selling to themselves, not knowing or trying to discover how their prospects would buy.

Million-dollar salespeople have an uncanny ability for sizing their prospects up. They can pick up *behavioral cues* that indicate how their prospects make buying decisions. They know what their prospects will say or how they will act in a given sales situation. They use these behavioral cues to get to know the prospect almost as well as he knows himself.

Even when these big-hitters were told of the unique and incredible techniques they had developed, they denied it. Very few of them realized how sophisticated in sales they really were.

Without knowing it, these men and women have mastered the techniques of subliminal selling. By modeling your behavior on theirs, you can have the same results they have.

Perceiving Predictable Behavior

The following short quiz may help you recognize just how predictable people's behavior can be. Take out a piece of paper and write down your answers.

- Think of a number between 1 and 10.
- What is your favorite flower?
- What is your favorite color?

I'll wager that you wrote down 3 or 4 for your number, chose rose for your flower, and blue for your favorite color. In fact, both my empirical evidence gathered after two years of lecturing to more than 300 groups averaging 200 people each and research performed by New York City psychologist Jacob Jacoby, Ph.D. (which he reported in a 1983 speech to the American Psychology Association) suggest that these answers come up about 93 percent of the time.

People *can* be very predictable. Through observation, you can predict and control your prospects' behavior. After reading *Subliminal Selling Skills*, you will be able to observe people so well that you too will be able to control your prospects' behavior patterns. But you will also be sophisticated enough to sell your prospects what they need in the way they want to buy.

CHAPTER 1

Your
Prospect's
Mental Map

Each of us has a unique mental map: that unique blueprint that details how we think, react, and make decisions. Very likely, you don't yet know how your prospect thinks. The problem is that if you don't know what your prospect's mental map looks like, you're only communicating information, not getting your message through to him. When you begin to understand your prospect's mental map, you will know how to communicate the right messages.

When you communicate the right messages, your prospect understands the meaning and intent of your ideas. He grasps the meaning *to him* of what you are saying as well as the intent behind your words. When he understands the meaning of your words and your intentions, he develops more rapport with you. When he has more rapport, he feels more trust.

Charting Your Prospect's Mental Map

People buy from you when they trust you. *To earn your prospect's trust, you must know him almost as well as he knows himself.*

If you don't understand what your prospect's unique mental map looks like, you may be selling by accident: You happen to say the right words at the right time and your prospect goes for it. Your prospect says okay, and you have the good sense to stop talking.

Here's a sentence for you. If you can, write it down; otherwise ingrain it by rote in your memory:

> If you can see John Smith through John Smith's eyes,
> You will sell John Smith what John Smith buys.

John Smith buys a lot from people who see him through his eyes, because John develops trust more easily with salespeople who see the world as he sees it.

Do you believe that? I think you'll find it to be true if you think hard about it.

You're going to start now to find out what John Smith's mental map looks like so that you can understand what and how John Smith buys and how to sell him what he wants. To begin with, to understand how John Smith buys, you must listen closely to him.

Neuro-Linguistic Programming: The Key to Your Prospect's Mental Map

Have you ever heard the statement that if you can get your prospect to see, hear, and feel your product idea, he will probably understand your product well enough to buy it?

Surprisingly enough, this concept is absolutely untrue, because prospective customers don't do all three of those things at once. They either *see* what you're saying, *hear* what you're saying, or *feel* what you're saying. But they may have trouble understanding all three different types of information at once. Presenting information in three ways may confuse them and irritate their perceived stability so that they will simply say no to you.

Richard Bandler and John Grinder, two psychological researchers once based at the University of California at Santa Cruz, tried to uncover whether the

HOW PEOPLE THINK

Visuals   Auditories   Kinesthetics

Source: Prepared by Kerry L. Johnson, Ph.D., International Productivity Systems, Inc., Box 1404, Tustin, Cal. 92681.

---

language people used had any relation to their thought processes.* While Bandler and Grinder's efforts were undertaken to help psychotherapists deal more effectively in resolving psychological problems, their research can also be used to help you understand how your prospects think.

These researchers, a psycho-linguist and a mathematician, spent years trying to look at the process by which patients and clients used language and the thought process behind that language. According to their research into what they call *neuro-linguistic programming (or NLP),* your prospects fit into one of three basic groups: visuals, auditories, or kinesthetics.

Visuals: Let the Image Do the Talking

Visuals are those individuals who understand more from what they see than from what they hear or feel. These people like brochures and colorful pictures— images that you verbally portray and paint for them while you talk.

Visuals take your words and translate them into pictures. If they can conjure

---

*Frogs Into Princes: Neuro-Linguistic Programming (Moab, Utah: Real People Press, 1979).

up an image while you talk to them, they comprehend much more quickly. If they can see your ideas while you communicate, they will understand much faster.

If you use language that prevents them from making quick pictures, you will lose rapport—and they will not buy.

Visuals make up the approximately 35 percent of your prospects who understand more from what they see than from what they hear or feel.

Auditories: It's Not What You Say, It's How You Say It

A second group of your prospects are called *auditories*. They buy not because of what they see or feel but because of how you talk about your products or ideas. They listen more closely to *how* you say things than to what you actually say.

Auditories care more about your vocal characteristics than the ideas you discuss. They are interested in your voice inflection, pace, pitch, rhythm, tone, and timbre.

Auditories make up approximately 25 percent of your prospect base. They will often buy more quickly over the telephone than they will face-to-face, because they may be more easily probed on the telephone and seeing you face-to-face can distract them.

Kinesthetics: Selling on the Gut Level

The third group of prospects falls into the *kinesthetic* category. Kinesthetics, who buy because of a "gut" feeling, make up approximately 40 percent of your prospective customers.

Kinesthetics:

- Buy because of a visceral feeling
- Establish trust as a result of the way they feel about you
- Form deep emotions about you
- Feel hot or cold about you very quickly
- Want to touch and feel your ideas
- Get goose bumps often
- Can feel their last shoulder massage
- Can experience deep emotions even while they're having a conversation with you

Operating
Out of a Primary Mode

Nobody is strictly a visual, auditory, or a kinesthetic, but everyone has a favorite central mode that he finds most comfortable to use. If you are right-handed, raise either hand right now. You probably raised the right one only because of comfort. You could have lifted your left, but it's just more awkward. The same is true of your primary mode: You can use the other two, but one is easier for you.

Discovering
If You Are Visual,
Auditory,
or Kinesthetic

Would you like to find your favorite mode? Here's a quick task you can do to determine whether you are a visual, auditory, or kinesthetic.

Try to find a partner—someone you know fairly well. Tell that person about your first hour of wakefulness this morning. Describe what happened.

While you talk, make sure you first discuss only what you *saw* this morning. When you're done with that, discuss what you *heard* this morning. And lastly, describe what you *felt* this morning.

You will quickly recognize your favorite system by noting the words or images you use to describe your first hour after waking up. Visuals remember pictures best, auditories things they heard, and kinesthetics what they felt.

Unfortunately, you can't ask all your prospects to tell you about their first hour of wakefulness. Nonetheless, you probably realize that if salespeople could find out your primary mode of thought, they could quickly establish rapport and trust. If they could gain your rapport and trust, they could also sell you much faster and increase their closing rate by helping you buy what you want.

Remember, people don't buy words, they buy trust.

- Visuals trust most quickly by seeing pictures.
- Auditories trust from hearing the right sounds.
- Kinesthetics trust from their gut.

How to Recognize Your Primary Communication Mode

No matter what your primary mode, you are, of course, able to see, hear, and feel if you have to. You have the ability to go into any mode you want, although some modes won't always be comfortable for you.

To get a feel for the mode you best fit into, try taking the three orientation tests shown in Exhibits 1, 2, and 3. Give yourself one point for every yes answer, zero points for every no answer. Then add up the total score. The test with the highest score is most likely our primary mode.

Be aware that if you are visual, you may be less effective in selling to auditories and kinesthetics; but by becoming more flexible with your prospects, you'll still be able to increase your sales and your profits. You'll also be more effective in dealing with people who do not have the same primary communication mode as you do.

I sat in on a meeting where a financial services salesman was trying to sell a couple his product. I recognized very quickly that he was alienating the wife. The salesman was slightly aware of human behavior and people skills, and had established very high rapport with the husband. But the wife was kinesthetic and the salesperson's predicates included visual words:

> How does this *look* to you, John? Can you get the
> *picture* of how your assets will be protected using this
> method? What do you *see* your future earning power
> being?

Needless to say, the salesman did not make a sale; the wife sabotaged him because she didn't feel comfortable with him. If the salesman had known what you know now, he would have talked to the husband in visual terms and to the wife in kinesthetic terms. He would have said to the husband:

> John, how does this *look* to you?

and to the wife:

> Kathryn, how do you *feel* about this?

And he would have continued in that vein:

> John, do you *see* how this will fit into your overall investment portfolio?

EXHIBIT 1. *Visual Orientation Test.*

_____ 1. I enjoy art galleries and window shopping.

_____ 2. I was good at spelling in school.

_____ 3. My confidence increases when I look good.

_____ 4. I would rather be shown an illustration than have something explained to me.

_____ 5. I find myself evaluating others based on their appearance.

_____ 6. I like to watch television and go to the movies.

_____ 7. It's important that my car is kept clean, inside and out.

_____ 8. I enjoy "people watching."

_____ 9. I often remember what someone looked like, but not his or her name.

_____ 10. I enjoy photography.

_____ 11. I enjoy speakers more if they use visual aids.

_____ 12. I am good at finding my way by using a map.

_____ 13. It's important that my house is clean and tidy.

_____ 14. I make a list of things I need to do each day.

_____ TOTAL

(Prepared by Kerry L. Johnson, Ph.D., International Productivity Systems, Inc., Box 1404, Tustin, Cal. 92681.)

EXHIBIT 2. *Auditory Orientation Test.*

_____ 1. I love to listen to music.
_____ 2. I would rather take an oral test than a written test.
_____ 3. I've been told I have a great voice.
_____ 4. I can resolve problems more quickly when I talk out loud.
_____ 5. I can usually determine someone's sincerity by the sound of his or her voice.
_____ 6. I would rather listen to cassettes than read books.
_____ 7. I can hear even the slightest noise my car makes.
_____ 8. Others tell me that I'm easy to talk to.
_____ 9. I am aware of what voices sound like on the phone, as well as face-to-face.
_____ 10. I often find myself humming or singing to the radio.
_____ 11. I would rather have an idea explained to me than to read it.
_____ 12. I am a good listener.
_____ 13. I like a house with rooms that allow for quiet areas.
_____ 14. I like to try to imitate the way people talk.

_____   TOTAL

(Prepared by Kerry L. Johnson, Ph.D., International Productivity Systems, Inc., Box 1404, Tustin, Cal. 92681.)

EXHIBIT 3. *Kinesthetic Orientation Test.*

_____   1. I feel compelled to dance to good music.

_____   2. I tend to answer test questions using my "gut" feelings.

_____   3. I enjoy being touched.

_____   4. I find myself holding or touching things as they are being explained.

_____   5. The way others shake hands with me means a lot to me.

_____   6. I like hiking and other outdoor activities.

_____   7. I like a car that feels good when I drive it.

_____   8. I tend to touch people when talking.

_____   9. I can't remember what people look like.

_____   10. I like to make things with my hands.

_____   11. I like to participate in activities rather than watch.

_____   12. I feel positive or negative toward others, sometimes without knowing why.

_____   13. I exercise because of the way I feel afterwards.

_____   14. I like a house that feels comfortable.

_____   15. I've been told that I'm well coordinated.

_____   TOTAL

(Prepared by Kerry L. Johnson, Ph.D., International Productivity Systems, Inc., Box 1404, Tustin, Cal. 92681.)

Kathryn, I would like to know your *impression* of the usefulness of this investment in your portfolio.

If the salesman had watched the words he used to each of his prospects, he would probably have made that sale.

When you talk to a prospect, you should communicate in his buying mode, not yours. Chapters 2, 3, and 4 show you how to uncover your prospect's primary communication mode so that you can get the most profitable results. Once you uncover his primary mode, you can use the subliminal selling techniques detailed in Chapters 5 through 15 to gain rapport with visuals, auditories, and kinesthetics and, as a result, generate more sales.

CHAPTER 2

Visuals

Visuals are people who understand what you say by what they see. Their minds work like a picture book encyclopedia. They turn everything you say into pictures. They make images and visions while you talk to them. When you discuss your ideas in pictures, they smile, their eyes glow, they understand, they comprehend.

Visuals' minds work like viewmasters. When you were younger, you probably at one time put one of these binocular-looking things up to your face. It had circular slides in it. When you pushed the lever you saw gorgeous photos—usually panoramas—in 3D.

When you talk to them, they start clicking the viewmasters in their brains. They try to understand your words by comparing both the pictures they remember and the pictures they are creating while you talk. They access images the whole time you talk.

Are you better with faces than with names? That is a very visual characteristic.

Knowing a Visual by the Eyes

You can tell a visual is making pictures because he typically moves his eyes wildly while you talk.

Basically, a visual does one of three things with his eyes:

1. He looks directly up and to the right when he thinks about future information in an effort to construct and create pictures. You may ask a prospect, "How much money do you estimate your business will make next year?" If he looks up right, he may be thinking, "I wonder if we can hit $6 million." He's actually creating a number on a sheet of mental paper.

2. He moves his eyes directly up and to the left when thinking about past information. This is how your prospect recalls pictures. If you ask, "How many units did you order last time," and he looks up left, he may be recalling a number from a sheet of paper on his desk or searching his photographic memory banks for an answer.

3. He looks straight ahead and his eyes appear to be unfocused as if he is staring off into space. Have you ever noticed when you are trying to make a sale that your prospect sometimes appears to be looking right through you? His eyes are glazed? He gives you a blank stare?

You were probably taught that if your prospect didn't make eye contact, he wasn't paying attention. That's simply not true. If someone looks through you, then looks into your eyes, he has simply translated and snythesized your words into images and pictures he can understand.

Finding Truth in the Eyes

Would you like to learn a quick technique to determine if your prospects are lying? The CIA is now using this technique to discover whether a paid informant is really telling the truth. For example, an agent may ask for information about where hostages are being held: "Have you noticed anything about that house? Have you seen Hezbollah members or Islamic Jihad there?" Those agents know that if the informant—especially if he displays visual characteristics—looks up and to the right, he is creating images of the future. Therefore, when he's asked about things he's seen in the past and looks up right into the future, he may be creating a lie; but if he looks up left, he's probably telling the truth.

However, people are not always lying when they look up right. Sometimes they look up right when they are unsure; or they may be constructing an estimate.

VISUAL'S EYES

up right

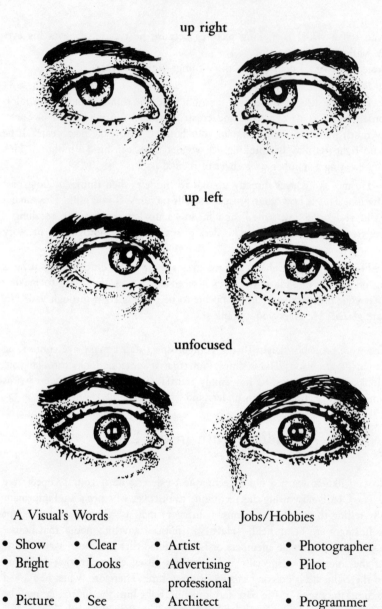

up left

unfocused

A Visual's Words		Jobs/Hobbies	
• Show	• Clear	• Artist	• Photographer
• Bright	• Looks	• Advertising professional	• Pilot
• Picture	• See	• Architect	• Programmer

Source: Prepared by Kerry L. Johnson, Ph.D., International Productivity Systems, Inc., Box 1404, Tustin, Cal. 92681.

Still, when you ask someone his name or where he is from and he looks up and to the right, you may wish to probe a little more deeply.

A Visual's Vocabulary

Many psychologists believe that everything people say indicates how they think. When people use visual words, they are thinking in pictures. Your prospects don't use random language. Their picture words indicate picture thoughts. Visuals use specific words that are giveaways to finding their mental map.

Even on the telephone, they will let you know that they are visuals by using words such as:

- *perspective.*
    "Well, let's keep this in *perspective.*"

- *show.*
    "Can you *show* it to me?"

- *bright.*
    "That's a pretty *bright idea.*"

- *picture.*
    "I can *picture* that."

- *clear.*
    "It's pretty *clear* so far."

- *looks.*
    "It *looks* good."

- *see.*
    "I *see* what you're saying."

- *view.*
    "Let me give you my *view* about that."

If you remember these words and remember that they indicate a visual thinker, I guarantee that during the course of your sales career, you will be able to use this information to your advantage whenever you meet with a prospect who thinks in a visual mode.

VISUAL CHARACTERISTICS

- Eye contact
- Voice high-pitched, fast
- Good visual memory

- Affected by color
- Good with directions

Source: Prepared by Kerry L. Johnson, Ph.D., International Productivity Systems, Inc., Box 1404, Tustin, Cal. 92681.

The Importance of Eye Contact for Visuals

Have you ever heard in a sales training program or elsewhere that you must maintain good eye contact with your prospect?

Well, visuals are the only people who care about eye contact. Auditories and kinesthetics may not even notice!

A visual person may say:

> I can see just by looking in your eyes that you're a
> sincere guy. I get a lot of trust from you. Just by eye
> contact I can tell you're an honest man.

If you are a nonvisual, however, you may never have understood what that meant before, or just what those visuals are looking at when they look at people's eyes.

Years ago, in a basic sales psychology course, I was taught that when a prospect doesn't make eye contact, he is not paying attention. That is simply not true. If a prospect breaks eye contact for long periods of time, he may be showing you disinterest or shyness; but if he looks away for a short period and then looks back at you, or if his eyes become glazed and he gives you a blank stare and then makes eye contact again, he is simply synthesizing pictures. He is comparing your words to what he is seeing on his mental map, translating your words into photographs and forming images in his head.

Visuals and Memory

Visuals have great visual memories. In fact, these people are probably better at spelling than most other people.

Were you good at spelling in school? Were you very, *very* good at spelling? If so, chances are that you constructed words by looking at each single letter in your mind—you could actually picture the whole word.

People who are bad at spelling probably think of words auditorially. They hear how a word should sound, and because they hear it phonetically, they misspell.

Would you like your child to be more adept at spelling? If your son or daughter is a visual, he or she may already be very effective in spelling bees. On the other hand, if your child is an auditory, he probably hears words. He may try to spell words phonetically, frequently misspelling even simple ones.

The next time your child spells a word, ask him to look up at the ceiling while he spells it. This artificial technique forces your child to see the word instead of hearing it. It may help him picture the way the word looks instead of hearing how it sounds. It will allow your child visually to remember rules like, i before e except after c.

Color

We are all deeply affected by color. Do you think it may influence your own perceptions? Which color Porsche seems to go faster, red or brown? Doesn't it seem as if red cars are quicker? Porsche dealers say that red models sell better than any other color. On the other hand, which pickup truck is more sturdy, brown or red? Everyone knows that brown trucks last longer, right? General Motors dealers report that consumers really believe this.

A few years ago, University of California researchers performed an amazing experiment. They went into a California prison and videotaped prison guards doing exercise curls with dumbbells. Sometime in your life you may have done a bit of weight lifting. A dumbbell is basically a small barbell for each hand. Prison guards are typically large-build men who usually are not allowed to wear guns in prisons. Instead they are so big that they defend themselves with nightsticks in case of riots.

In the study, on camera, one prison guard did twenty-eight curls without stopping. A dark blue poster board was then placed in front of him.

Guess how many curls the guard did?

If you guessed more, you are absolutely right. Even though you'd have thought fatigue would have set in, the prison guard did more curls; twenty-nine in fact.

The researchers then exchanged the blue poster board for a pink one and again asked the guard to do curls.

Guess how many he did this time—more or fewer?

If you guessed fewer, you are absolutely right. He did twenty-eight with no color, twenty-nine with blue, and his score dropped all the way down to five curls with pink.

The California prison system is now using pink in certain cells called sedation cells. When a prisoner goes crazy, or becomes rampant and violent, he is put into a pink cell for thirty minutes. According to reports, the color pink has an enormously effective and calming influence on the hostile prisoner.

There are actually two ways that color affects behavior:

1. *Physiologically.* There are some colors that cause people direct eye and retina irritation.
2. *Psychologically.* Your prospect associates the color with an experience he has had in the past.

Certain colors have the ability to cause your prospect either a high comfort level in a sales situation or discomfort. These colors tend to have an enormous influence over your prospect's behavior.

Several experts* now agree that these are the three best colors to use with your prospects, not only as far as clothing is concerned but when you are preparing your brochures, stationary, and any other collateral material.

1. *Blue.* The best color to use is the favorite color of both men and women in the United States. In fact, it also happens to be part of IBM's nickname, "Big Blue." You don't really think that at an IBM board meeting decades ago some vice-president said to the company founder, "Hey, this is my favorite color. Why not make our company logo *blue?*"

IBM realized that blue would have an enormous influence over its product buyers, so it chose that color for the logo. IBM wanted to appeal to executives who might purchase expensive computer systems.

2. *Dove-gray.* The second-best color happens to be a color in which most major U.S. airports are painted. Many hub airline terminals are very competitive. They cater to executive travelers of upper socioeconomic status, who fly more frequently than anyone else. It has been found that these executives are highly attracted to *dove-gray.*

---

*See Suggested Reading at the end of this book, especially Caudill, Costigan, Johnson, and Tysee.

3. *Hunter green.* The third-best color is one that is particularly effective to use when you promise a very heavy investment return or revenue. This color is bound to influence your prospect. *Hunter green* causes most people to think of money and U.S. currency. Prudential-Bache Securities has presented its Rock Solid, Market Wise advertising slogan over a hunter green background.

There are also colors that are practically guaranteed to make your prospects uncomfortable. From a psychological standpoint, the three worst colors in the spectrum are ones your prospects quickly associate with negativity: black, purple, and yellow.

Perhaps the worst of the three is the color that affected *U.S. News* reporter Nicholas Daniloff when he was kidnaped by the KGB and kept in a cell painted in this color for two solid weeks during interrogation. The KGB agents realized that they could not physically harm Daniloff because of negative world opinion, so instead they tried to torture him psychologically, and possibly even brainwash him, by using only this one color in his cell. It is a color that causes depression within just a few short minutes of constant eye contact. It is a color most quickly associated in America with death and dying. The color is *black.* (Interestingly enough, the Chinese funereal color is the opposite of black: white.)

The next-worst color is the color interculturally identified with sickness, nausea, and vomiting. In fact, Japan's Kabuki dancers even use it in their shows to indicate death or sickness. The audience knows that when a dancer comes on stage with this color headband, he will not be back in the next scene because of the character's death by sickness. The U.S. military has even designated this color for a wartime medal, which is in the shape of a heart. And if you're Catholic, you probably know that during Lent, this color vestment is draped over the cross as a sign of mourning. The color is *purple.*

The third-worst color is the most insidious of the three. This color will increase anxiety levels within forty-five seconds and will increase blood pressure nearly as fast. The color happens to be the most irritating to the retina of an individual over fifty years old. A few years back, however, the color was surprisingly *The Wall Street Journal's* recommended power-tie color for the year. The color is *yellow.*

While not being one of the three worst colors, *red* is also a bad color to use with prospects. One of the reasons behind this is largely that in our society, red is associated with fire as in fire engine, danger as in police, stop as in stop signs, and blood.

Years ago, a physician I know had occasion to speak to an antiabortion audience. She talked about how abortion was handled in different societies and also talked about its perils. However, she made one great mistake: She wore a red dress. Although she made a very good case for antiabortion practices, the dress affected the audience so negatively that many people walked out on her presentation.

The audience had associated her red clothing with blood, blood with murder, and murder with abortion. The physician had been advertising abortion psychologically by the color of her dress.

Color can even affect your appetite level. Would you like a quick tip on how to lose weight? A color that actually increases your appetite also increases your metabolism. Interestingly, while people associate red with negativity and blue with positive associations, when it comes to food, the colors seem to have an opposite effect. Red will increase your appetite, while the blue decreases it. Ever hear of blue food? You never will (even blueberries are not really blue). So if you are trying to lose weight, blue place mats and napkins may decrease your appetite, while red place settings are best to avoid.

With all the current talk of dressing for success, the bottom line with colors in business situations is for a man to wear a dark blue (or gray) suit and with a hunter-green tie when meeting with prospects who earn over $40,000. If at all possible, he should avoid black suits and anything purple.

Keep in mind that visuals are much more influenced by colors than nonvisuals are. Auditories and kinesthetics would probably not even be aware of what you are wearing in business situations. They would simply know that you had a voice, were somewhere between 5 and 7 feet tall, and were wearing a suit or a dress.

Using Image to Increase Your Production

Visuals are self-conscious about their and others' appearance. Nonvisuals may simply not notice, but visuals are extremely aware.

It may seem like pretty silly stuff, but your image is a key to whether or not you gain rapport with your prospect, particularly if he is a visual. You want to avoid letting your prospect see anything odd about your clothing—any dissymmetry. Some people you will come in contact with will become distracted from your sales presentation because they have problems with your image.

Image experts believe that well-tailored clothing commands respect. They also believe that cheap, ill-fitting clothing causes lost sales. Appearance means a lot, particularly to your visual prospects. Kinesthetics may be more affected by a visceral feeling than by your appearance, but when you meet with a client, it's best to take every precaution against not offending him with your appearance.

The Simple Tie

Many sharp businesspeople already know that a man's tie may make a difference when it comes to sales. But have you paid much attention to the ties men wear? This simple clothing accessory may also play a role in helping a man gain acceptance from his prospects, and if prospects accept him, he can translate that acceptance into higher rapport.

During the Renaissance, ties were worn by wealthy individuals as bibs during meals and as napkins after the meals were over. The tie has evolved from a utilitarian tool to a thin piece of material worn as an accessory.

It is important for a man to wear a tie correctly. Usually it should extend at least down to the belt, but in some areas of the country, it is fashionable to wear it 2 or 3 inches below the belt. The tie should be securely fastened at the neck in a Windsor knot.

The most accepted material for the tie today is silk. Most polyester/silk blends look like blends, and polyester ties look like polyester. If you can tell the difference between a silk and a polyester tie, so can your prospects. No volume discount on polyester ties can make up for the visual uneasiness that tie might give a man's prospect.

The five most popular styles of ties are:

1. The rep, or diagonally striped tie
2. The foulard
3. The club
4. The polka-dot
5. The solid tie

Bow ties, except when worn with tuxedos or by graphic artists or architects whose jobs make them more practical, are infrequently worn by sales professionals.

The most universally accepted and useful tie is the rep, which at one time, identified the wearer's military rank. It is important that the colors of the striped rep tie not blend together but be distinctly separate. Rep ties are widely accepted because they can be worn when a salesman does business with either blue-collar workers or professionals. Visually, it has less of an air of snobbishness than other ties and will be accepted by a wide variety of prospects.

The foulard—typically featuring small circles or triangles on a woven silk background—has become the Ivy League look of the 1980s. The style originated in the Northeast where, originally, only the most wealthy wore them. If he has an appointment with a CEO, an owner of a fairly large company, or a highly affluent professional, the salesman may score extra points by wearing a foulard.

I once spoke to a Young President's Organization meeting. I carefully dressed in my well-pressed, conservative blue three-piece suit. My black English-toed shoes were freshly shined. After my presentation, I was complemented on my tie by one of the attendees. I had chosen to wear a foulard to the meeting. I thanked him, looked around the room, and noticed that most of the meeting attendees were also wearing foulards. I had been complemented because I had worn the same tie as the rest of the attendees and visually matched my audience. People trust people who are similar to themselves both in behavior and in appearance.

A club tie has repeating figures evenly spaced across it on a solid background. The figures usually depict such things as sailboats, tennis rackets, ducks, college buildings, or even corporate logos. The club tie is typically an upper-middle-class tie, reserved for those who have a common interest.

A tie featuring figures that are appealing to your prospect will surely pique his interest. But if it has squash rackets on it and the client's idea of exercise is watching Hulk Hogan wrestle on television, believe me, it won't help score any extra points.

Obviously, most professionals want their products or services to be the topic of conversation, not their ties. But they can help gain rapport by choosing an appropriate tie. When I spoke to a group of insurance agents from New Jersey, I decided to sport an "I Love New Jersey" tie. It was an instant hit. The audience accepted me immediately.

The *polka dot* tie is the most formal of the business ties. The most traditional model consists of evenly spaced white dots on a navy blue background, but there are many variations. The most coordinated look is to wear a tie with dots that pick up the shirt color. Since the most common polka dot tie features white dots, the most conservative look would be to wear the tie with a white shirt. The smaller the dot, the more formal the tie.

The best tie for a man with a limited wardrobe is a *solid-color* tie. Navy and maroon shades are must-have colors, gray and brown are backups. The solid-color tie is not as formal as the polka dot or foulard tie, but it presents the correct visual image for selling to middle-class prospects. Solid colors go visually well with striped shirts and more casual clothing. It is frequently worn by retail salespeople.

A man may lose his air of sophistication if he wears a solid-color tie when selling to affluent prospects. But a lower- or middle-income client may be intimidated by a foulard or polka dot tie. Remember that a person's visual appearance should be one that helps gain acceptance and build rapport with the target audience.

Therefore, for men: The next time you pick a tie, remember that, particularly with your visual prospects for whom appearance is so important, it may have a bearing on the level of rapport you gain. Wearing the right tie at the

HOW TO SEDUCE VISUALS

1. Use visual predicates.
2. Watch what you wear.
3. Let them see your ideas.
4. Use gestures.

Source: Prepared by Kerry L. Johnson, Ph.D., International Productivity Systems, Inc., Box 1404, Tustin, Cal. 92681.

right time may give you an edge in developing rapport more quickly with prospects. We develop rapport with those who are like us in both visual appearance and behavior.

How to Seduce a Visual

To persuade visuals effectively—to literally communicate and sell visuals the way they want to be sold—you should:

1. *Use visual words.* Remember the visual-based words I mentioned before—words such as "show," "clear," "bright," "picture," and "see"? Your visual sales prospects want you to talk to them precisely, using a visual vocabulary.

2. *Recognize when you are talking to a visual.* Remember, I gave you two ways to tell if your prospects are visuals: (1) Their eyes go up to the left or right or they stare blankly because they are creating visual pictures in their minds; (2) they themselves use visual-based words.

If you were talking to a CPA or an engineer, for example, chances are you could score points and gain higher rapport if he thought you knew his business. If you spoke to the CPA using terms such as "declining balance" and "depreciation schedules," he would think you knew what he was thinking. If you used analytic terms that the engineer typically uses every day in his life, he would also trust you as somebody who knew what he was experiencing.

The same thing is true with visuals. *If you use a visual's own words when you talk to him, he'll be convinced you know how he thinks.*

Here's how to talk to a visual prospect. Imagine you are selling real estate:

> Evan, can't you just *picture* your family all sitting
> together in this lovely dining room? I bet you can *see*
> how all your furniture will *look* when we fill up this
> room. Notice how *bright* it is with all of these
> windows? *See* what I mean?

A woman I know named Myra Rodriguez* makes more than $1 million a year in commissions selling financial products. Here's how she deals with her visual prospects. She asks,

> What do you *see* yourself accomplishing?

You can see the prospect's eyes go up to the ceiling as he pictures what he has in mind.

Joel, a partner in one of the Big Eight accounting firms, told me how he got one of the biggest accounts of the year for his company. Joel, who is based in Denver, received a call from a credit union executive asking him to speak to the credit union members on new tax proposals.

The credit union executive said,

> I'd like to *see* what you can offer. I'd like you to
> give me a *picture* of how you would do the presentation.
> I have interviewed numerous firms for this job, but I'd
> like to get your *perspective* on how you would handle
> the assignment before I use your company.

Joel immediately recognized, even over the telephone, that the executive was obviously a visual who operated primarily in a visual mode. Joel quickly realized that not only would his accounting firm receive a great deal of business after the presentation because of the huge number of attendees who would be present but that he needed to use just the right words at the right time, not only to gain trust but to attract the interest of this executive who was in search of a convention speaker.

---

*While Myra Rodriguez is based on a real person, a fictitious name has been used. This is true of all the names used in examples throughout the text.

Joel asked the executive,

> Is there anything else you would like to *see*?

The executive responded,

> Yes, I'd like you to *show* me what your presentation
> would cover.

Joel was surprised by how much of a textbook visual this executive was, but he knew that to keep his interest and close on the speaking engagement, he would have to continue focusing on the executive's visual mode. Joel said,

> Well, we use gorgeous blue handouts with gold borders,
> giving the attendees something they can take home to
> *see* from the presentation. We also use a projection
> system that transfers vivid numbers in graphs from a
> computer onto a screen. This will dazzle the attendees'
> *eyes*. We will also make this very simple so that the
> attendees can *see* how much they can benefit from these
> government tax proposals and get a *perspective* of how
> their businesses will profit with the presentation.

Joel told me that the executive excitedly said over the phone to him,

> I can *see* that; I can *see* that!

Joel asked, when the union executive would like to follow up. The executive responded quickly,

> I was going to interview other firms for this
> assignment, but I have such a good *picture* that you
> will do a great job, I think you're the one.

Had Joel not realized that this executive was a visual, the rapport over the phone would have quickly been lost. Joel would not have received one of his biggest clients of the year.

One of the biggest sales hitters I know masterfully seduces his visual prospects by using props so they can visually see what he is talking about. He does millions of dollars of business each year using the simplest, most unsophisticated technique I've ever heard of: He talks about forced savings plans, using a pie as a visual aid. He'll say,

> Mr. Prospect, right now you're paying this much in
> taxes. . . .

and he'll slice the pie to show Mr. Prospect just how much less he could be paying. The funny thing is that by using this method, the salesperson doesn't have to work very hard, because *he gets his prospects to see the concept so clearly that they understand it twice as fast.*

Another important point to remember when selling to visuals: *Use your hands when you talk to them.* Get them to see things by painting pictures for them in the air, not just on paper. If you do, you're likely to get more business.

Here's a method one disability insurance agent uses. When talking with a married man who's considering buying insurance, he'll say,

> What do you think the *expression* on your wife's face
> will *look* like when you *show* her that if something
> happens to you she'll have $8,000 a month coming in?
> What do you think she'll *look* like? Can't you just *see*
> the relief on her face?

The prospect won't be able to see anything but a happy look on his wife's face. He'll look up and to the right, constructing a picture and a smile. He will visualize it and see the agent's point.

   3. *Keep brochures, graphs, and pictures in front of visuals constantly when you are selling to them.* You've already learned that visuals want to see certain colors— hunter green, blue, and dove-gray—when they look at visual illustrations. But you should also realize that *any concept will be understood and comprehended much more quickly if you can show the prospect a bar chart or a graph while you talk.*

The most productive and profit-producing salespeople in the country frequently use slides, even if they are presenting to only two or three prospects. While being careful not to darken the room for fear that the prospect will fall asleep, the salesperson will try to get the visual to see as much as possible in an effort to get that prospect to buy more quickly.

Overhead transparencies are a good, effective tool if used in the right way. Make sure, especially with a visual, that while you show a transparency, it is clearly in focus and also in color. Avoid using black-and-white transparencies for the obvious reason that black is significantly associated with death and dying and white may give your prospect a sense of snow-blindness and possibly irritate him because of the brightness of the overhead. More important, be sure to turn the overhead projector off before switching transparencies so your prospect won't see the projector's bright light when there's no transparency on it.

Remember: *If you can get your prospects to think in their most natural mode, they are going to buy much more quickly from you because you will gain their trust faster. You will communicate with intent and meaning and accomplish more business.*

CHAPTER 3

Auditories

Auditories are sound-based people who listen to the way you say things. They often get more information from how you say things than by what you show them, or even by what you say. The way you deliver information—your voice pitch, pace, and timbre—everything about your intonation, means more to them than your actual ideas. Auditories actually listen more to the delivery than the actual content of a statement.

You can deal daily with your auditory prospects, but to be effective and close sales, you don't really need to see them face-to-face. They can buy as readily over the telephone as by seeing you on an appointment.

Auditories sometimes even have amorous relationships over the telephone. It's not uncommon for auditory men and women to have a more romantic relationship over the telephone than they do face-to-face.

The Eyes of an Auditory

One way of knowing that you've got an auditory prospect is to look at his eyes. Remember how the visual will look up right or left or seem to be looking in a defocused manner straight through you? Well, auditories also give cues with their eyes that let you know they're thinking auditorially.

In each mode of communication, looking right is an indication that the person is thinking in the future. *When an auditory looks directly straight across and to the right, chances are he too is thinking about future information,* but in his case, he is thinking about or hearing future sounds. For example:

> I wonder what my wife will *say* to me when she *hears*
> that I've bought this [*computer or car or whatever the product may be*].

Or,

> I wonder what my accountant will *say. . . ."*

You can actually force a prospect to think auditorially if you want to. You can ask an auditory, for example,

> What will your wife *say* to you if you tell her how
> much you've saved on this product?

If that individual is really hearing you, he will look side right constructing the actual sounds of his wife's voice.

When you probe your prospect, you may ask questions such as,

> How much money do you expect to have in your budget
> next year?"

If the auditory looks side right he is probably constructing sounds as he is thinking.

Auditories will move their eyes side left when thinking about past information. If you asked a prospect a question such as, "How much money did you pay last year in taxes?" the auditory may look side left in an effort to remember a conversation he had with his accountant who told him exactly how much money he paid. He may even be trying to hear what his wife told him a few days ago.

You can also force someone to think auditorially by saying something like,

AN AUDITORY'S EYES

side right

side left

down left

<table>
<tr><td>**An Auditory's Words**</td><td>**Jobs/Hobbies**</td></tr>
</table>

An Auditory's Words		Jobs/Hobbies
• *Tone*	• *Rings*	• Musician
• *Static*	• *Sounds*	• Teacher
• *Hear*	• *Say*	• Telephone salesperson
		• Radio announcer

Source: Prepared by Kerry L. Johnson, Ph.D., International Productivity Systems, Inc., Box 1404, Tustin, Cal. 92681.

Have you ever *heard* a commercial on the radio?

It will force him to think in past sounds, and he will move his eyes side left.

The Auditory Vocabulary

Like visuals, auditories have a vocabulary of their own, which includes words such as:

- *tone.* "Don't take that *tone* with me, young man."
- *static.* "All I ever get from you is a lot of *static.*"
- *hear.* "Yeah, I *hear* what you're saying."
- *ring.* "Hey, that *rings* a bell."
- *sound.* "*Sounds* good to me."
- *say.* "*Say*, did you hear the one about the two ostriches?"
- *tell.* "Can you *tell* me more about it?"
- *talk.* "*Talk* to me further about this."

Auditory Characteristics

Auditories try to make their voices sound low, rhythmic, and smooth. They frequently have resonant or booming voices.

Some psychological researchers believe that you can determine whether somebody is thinking auditorially because he will touch his face as he listens to you. An auditory will frequently put his hand up to his face in an effort to hear what you are saying.

The next time you see someone talking to you with his hand up to his face, try to notice whether the eyes are positioned side right, side left, or down left. Listen for the vocabulary of an auditory.

Auditories are more aware of sounds, delivery, pace, pitch, and tone than are visuals or kinesthetics. They experience great joy from attending live concerts and listening to music.

If you gave an auditory a choice between a big-screen television set or stereo speakers on their existing regular-size television, they would choose the speakers. They would rather have the better sound coming out of the television than a better visual image.

Auditories love the telephone. They sometimes do more business over the telephone than in any other way because they love to hear themselves and others talk. Auditories listen so deeply to what you say that sometimes just the inflection of your voice can distract them. Because auditories themselves try very hard

AUDITORY CHARACTERISTICS

- Trying to sound good
- Voices lower, rhythmic, and smooth

- Like concerts and music
- Talk to themselves

Source: Prepared by Kerry L. Johnson, Ph.D., International Productivity Systems, Inc., Box 1404, Tustin, Cal. 92681.

---

to sound good almost all the time, they often speak rhythmically and deliberately, conscious of every word. (Visuals, on the other hand, speak very quickly. They are not concerned with how they sound at all. They are too busy making pictures in their mind and *seeing* how things are).

Visuals breath very high in the chest. They breath more shallowly and their voices are pitched higher than those of auditories. In fact, visuals often speak quickly because their minds operate like a movie camera, seeing each frame of the film flash by quickly and then talking (creating the soundtrack for their internal movie) just as fast.

Tonal Auditories

Another eye movement the auditory type may make is to look directly down and to the left. If you notice the behavior, you know you're dealing with a *tonal auditory:* those individuals who make sense of what you are saying by talking to themselves and having internal conversations.

Have you ever heard people who, when faced with an unpleasant task, start to mumble to themselves? This is also a sign of the tonal auditory.

When a tonal auditory looks down and to the left, he is actually thinking about what you are saying to him by trying to compare it with what he has heard before.

HOW TO SEDUCE AUDITORIES

1. Use auditory predicates.
2. Tickle their ears.
3. Play backround music.
4. Listen to yourself.
5. Explain illustrations.

Source: Prepared by Kerry L. Johnson, Ph.D., International Productivity Systems, Inc., Box 1404, Tustin, Cal. 92681.

He may be comparing your ideas to what he thinks he should be hearing. In a way, he is talking silently to himself. If you talk too, he won't hear you.

Unlike visuals, auditories don't create internal movies but, rather, like to talk to themselves. They can resolve problems better when they discuss things with themselves.

Psychologists used to think that talking to yourself was a sign of neurosis— even a sign of schizophrenia—until it was discovered that that behavior is an easy way to go through what is called self-talk: actually talking out events to solve problems more quickly and effectively.

How to Seduce an Auditory

While we all operate in visual, auditory, or kinesthetic modes from time to time, each of us favors one mode over the others. There are several techniques you can use when you are dealing with prospects who are primarily auditory. The best technique is to use auditory words.

How does this *sound* so far?

Does this *ring* a bell with you, Mr. Prospect?

And please, if you're selling a product that has auditory qualities, sell the prospect on those qualities.

Here's an illustration from real estate: Let's say you were selling a house with a creek passing through the backyard. To the auditory prospect, you would want to stress how nice the creek sounds.

Or if you were selling refrigerators, you would stress how quiet a particular model is.

Or for a car:

> Listen to the way this engine hums.

If you are aware of your prospect's thought mode, you will be able to use the right words. If you are not, you may mismatch.

The Seductive Nature of Music

Music affects your prospect's behavior patterns and emotional attitude. Do you see more clearly when the music is on or off? If you said off, you're right. Music may influence auditories more than visuals or kinesthetics.

A Loyola University study has reported that music can even affect supermarket sales.* Do you think people buy more when the music is fast or slow? If you guessed slow, you are absolutely right.

The report claims that supermarket sales are 38.2 percent higher when slow, easy-listening music is played in a store. But when he asked shoppers what they thought of the music inside, 33 percent said they didn't know what kind of music was playing and 39 percent denied that there was any music playing at all.

Corporate America has used music to influence people for years. The Muzak Corporation says that its music can increase factory productivity by 17 percent, and claims it can increase clerical performance in the office by 13.5 percent. Muzak also claims to reduce turnover by 53 percent.

One of the reasons why we buy more when slower music is played is because of the *impulse factor*. In department stores, as well as in supermarkets, we typically go in to buy a very specific product, such as cosmetics or food. When the background music is fast, we tend to move and think more quickly about what we want to buy. As a result, we exit the store more quickly.

But the impulse factor kicks in when slower music is played. Easy-listening music not only tends to slow down the shopper's pace and allow him to think about what he came in to buy, it also lets his mind drift, so that he looks at other products rather than running out the door. At this easy-going pace, he

---

*See Suggested Reading at the end of this book, especially Carter and McLoughlin.

may see something he likes and buy it impulsively, thereby increasing overall store sales.

James Keenan, a psychological researcher at Fairfield University in Connecticut (who coincidentally sits on Muzak's Board of Scientific Advisors) discovered that Muzak works best when popular, light-music selections are programmed in ascending order of stimulus progression. This means that the music's pace gradually quickens as time goes on during the day. On clerical tests, workers perform more accurately and faster when the Muzak is programmed this way.

In their book *Super Learning* (Dell, 1982), Sheila Ostrander and Lynn Schroeder prescribe baroque music to help readers learn and retain more information. Ostrander and Schroeder have discovered that baroque music apparently helps to relax and calm the mind. This in turn helps readers to absorb more.

Helen Bonnie, founder and director of the music therapy department of Catholic University of America in Washington, D.C., has found an interesting effect when sedate, classical or baroque music is played in hospitals. Her research in coronary care units shows that blood pressure actually decreases when patients are exposed to slow, sedate music.

Explaining What They See

Auditories like to have concepts explained to them verbally. When you use illustrations with auditories, you should show them a piece of paper or let them see an outline to gain a reference point; but then you should verbally explain the outline to them.

A Southern California salesperson I know mails an audiotape to prospects describing his company's background. The tape also includes testimonials from past clients. If such a tape gets into the hands of an auditory, it is likely to persuade him more easily. At least the tape helps the salesperson establish some credibility before he telephones the prospect.

Have you ever had a prospect who looked at your product brochure or illustration and just asked, "Can you please explain this to me?" Such a prospect is very likely to be an auditory.

Ann Chin, a financial planner in Orlando, Florida, told me a story where, after fifteen minutes of drawing pictures, diagrams, and graphs, her physician prospect said, "Ann, I don't want to see all of this. Just talk to me." Ann said, "If I don't show you how this investment works, you're not going to understand it." The doctor said, "Try me." Ann put her felt pen and visual aids down and verbally explained the concept. After ten minutes, the prospect crossed his arms, leaned back in his chair, closed his eyes, and smiled. Ann knew enough about body language to know that when people cross their arms, they are likely to be bored: When they lean back and close their eyes they are sleeping; when they smile as well, they are fantasizing. Offended, Ann abruptly blurted, "If you're going to fall asleep, we'll have to reschedule this." The prospect opened his eyes, leaned forward, and said, "Ann, how much money do I need to give you to get this started right now?" Her prospect was an auditory. He was more influenced by what he heard than by what he saw.

Haven't you ever closed your eyes upon hearing beautiful music? The physician wasn't sleeping, he was enjoying. But your prospects will not tell you how to sell them the way Ann's prospect did. If you can't read their mode of thought, they will not buy.

Further underscoring the way in which auditories process information, I have studied the eye movements of auditories when they are given outlines to read. Auditories will look at the words across the top of the page, look down the left side of the sheet, and glance at a few things in the middle of the sheet. But they will not continue to try to read the sheet or get more information from it.

Why? Because they get more information from what they hear from you than from what they see. So give the visual illustration or outline to the auditory and wait twelve seconds; then verbally explain what he has just looked at.

To get the kinds of results or behavior you'd like to receive from prospects, it's important to stay aware of the mode in which they operate.

CHAPTER 4

Kinesthetics

Kinesthetics are those individuals who really make decisions not by what they see or hear but by how they feel. They get information more from touch, feel, emotions, gut instincts, attitudes, and hunches than from the content of what you say.

Kinesthetics really need to get a physical or psychological sense about you before they can trust you. *Kinesthetics buy on the basis of how they feel when they are around you.*

The Kinesthetic's Eyes and Vocabulary

When kinesthetics feel deep emotions, they look down and to the right. When you are trying to determine whether or not your prospect is kinesthetic, remember: *Looking down to the right is your indication that someone is thinking kinesthetically.*
The words kinesthetics use face-to-face or on the telephone include:

- touch base. "Hey, let's *touch base* next week."
- handle. "Let me see if I can get a *handle* on that."

A KINESTHETIC'S EYES

down right

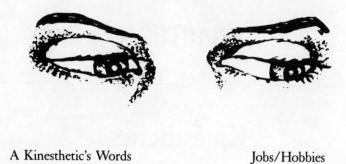

A Kinesthetic's Words   Jobs/Hobbies

- Touch base
- Handle
- Grab
- Rub
- Feel
- Impression

- Athlete
- Carpenter
- Cook
- Minister
- Sculptor
- Psychologist

Source: Prepared by Kerry L. Johnson, Ph.D., International Productivity Systems, Inc., Box 1404, Tustin, Cal. 92681.

- grab. "How does that *grab* you?"
- rub. "Well, it *rubs* me the wrong way."
- feel. "Here's how I *feel* about what you just said."

When your prospects use these or similar words, you know they are feeling as they speak.

Remember the visuals? They say things like, "Here's my *view.*" The auditories say, "Here's how it *sounds* to me." Kinesthetics, on the other hand, will say, "Here's my *feeling* on the subject"; "I've got a good *grasp* on that"; or "Here's my *impression.*"

Understanding Kinesthetic Thinking

Someone once told me that he didn't like selling to kinesthetics because he thought they "didn't think in the right way." But there is no "right" or "wrong" way to think. Similarly, there is no right or wrong way to sell, as long as you sell the way your prospect wants to buy. The sooner you understand what your

prospect is thinking and the mode in which he thinks, the faster you can appeal
to him in a way that he will find irresistible.

This same person told me that he thought kinesthetics were slower thinkers,
not intellectually bright people. That is simply not true. Albert Einstein was
probably a kinesthetic. If you look at old news footage of Einstein being inter-
viewed, you will notice that when asked about his theories, his eyes go down to the
right. He rarely makes eye contact with the camera. Einstein came up with the
theory of relativity in the space of two hours by imagining what it might *feel* like to
ride a bolt of lightning through the universe. He *felt* the theory of relativity.

Kinesthetic people think differently from the way others think, not necessarily more slowly.

Recognizing Kinesthetics

Remember the televised debates between Geraldine Ferraro and George Bush—
that great knock-down, drag-out boxing match they called the vice-presidential
debates? The consensus among newscasters was that Bush was the more charismatic and articulate in front of the television camera, although many analysts
believe that Ferraro appeared to be better-informed about the issues.

Ferraro, however, made some big mistakes in front of the camera. When
reporters directed questions to Bush, he would look directly into the camera,
become unfocused, and stare blankly like a visual while he thought of an answer.
When he came up with his answer, he continued to look directly into the
camera. The television viewing audience never saw Bush breaking eye contact
with them. But Ferraro, like a true kinesthetic, looked down to the right and
completely lost eye contact with the cameras. After each question was asked,
she looked down at the podium. At one point, the viewing audience heard Dan
Rather of CBS television ask why she was looking down so much. Morely Safer
answered, "I don't know, Dan. There aren't any notes in front of her. Nothing
to look at."

She wasn't reading anything. She was just functioning like a kinesthetic.
Undoubtedly, that was the only way she could think—by looking down to the
right. Then, she'd look back up to the camera and answer the question. The
problem was that the viewers didn't understand her thought processes. They
thought Ferraro might be trying to hide something because she looked down so
much, breaking eye contact.

What type do you think former President Jimmy Carter is? Think about it.
Visual? Auditory? Kinesthetic? Imagine Carter in that warm cardigan sweater,
hosting one of his chats in front of a crackling fire in the hearth. If you watched
him with reporters, he'd reach out and touch them. He had town hall lectures

KINESTHETIC CHARACTERISTICS

- Feeling hot or cold about you
- Frequent pauses in conversation
- Liking to TOUCH people and things

Source: Prepared by Kerry L. Johnson, Ph.D., International Productivity Systems, Inc., Box 1404, Tustin, Cal. 92681.

---

because he wanted to reach out and touch the people of America. He's a kinesthetic, and he used kinesthetic words, as in,

> Here's my *feeling* about that.

Kinesthetic Characteristics

Kinesthetics have certain characteristics that will let you identify them easily.

1. *Kinesthetics feel hot or cold about you very quickly.* They make more judgments about you in the first four minutes of meeting you than someone else does in two or three weeks. If you are trying to sell something to a kinesthetic, it's very important for you to establish their primary mode of thinking up-front in your dealings.

2. *Kinesthetics make frequent pauses in their conversations.* Have you ever had the following kind of exchange?

SALESMAN: Loren, I'd like to know what you think about this personal computer system so far.

LOREN [*slowly*]: Well, Kerry, I think that, ah, what you're saying to me right now has a lot of ah, ah, merit, and frankly, that, ah, I feel that I have a good grasp on how it works, ah. . . .

Do you know people who talk like Loren? Do you know what they're doing? They're trying to get a feeling. They're asking themselves,

> How do I *feel* about what he just said?

And, when they get their feeling, they keep on talking, frequently pausing when they speak. That's just how their minds work.

3. *Kinesthetics love to touch people and things.* They want to touch you if they possibly can. In fact, they can sometimes get more information from what they can touch and feel than from what they hear or see. Kinesthetics may touch you to make a point—on the arm, on the shoulder, on the back.

4. *Kinesthetics can understand, perceive, and comprehend your ideas much faster when they are made to feel good.* Almost every meeting planner and program chairman in America knows that if a room is too cold, the audience will have trouble listening to the speaker. Similarly, if a room is too hot, people may fall asleep or at least complain about the heat. *Kinesthetics are likely to feel temperature changes more quickly than visuals or auditories.*

Another thing you can do to make your prospect feel better about you has nothing to do with temperature. If you visit your prospect's place of business or home and he tries to make you feel comfortable, you should accept his offers of hospitality to make him feel good about being a good host.

On many interviews when I have accompanied a salesperson and the prospect has offered us a cup of coffee, cola, water, or even a couple of cookies, I have seen the salesperson initially refuse the offer. This is a mistake. By accepting the prospect's hospitality, the salesperson is saying,

> I respect you; I enjoy being here; I would like
> to partake of your graciousness.

By not accepting the hospitality, the prospect, trying to be gracious, has his best intentions thrown back in his face and automatically *feels* uncomfortable at having this guest in his house or office.

Friends readily accept coffee, cola, or even a beer. Why must the salesperson be different? Make the prospect feel good. If he is able to be a good host, he is

HOW TO SEDUCE KINESTHETICS

1. Use kinesthetic predicates.
2. Give them things to touch.

Source: Prepared by Kerry L. Johnson, Ph.D., International Productivity Systems, Inc., Box 1404, Tustin, Cal. 92681.

---

more likely to feel comfortable with you, and when he's comfortable, you have established rapport.

How to Seduce a Kinesthetic

Here's how to work with kinesthetics to have maximum effectiveness with them in a sales situation.

Recognize that they want you to use kinesthetic words. They want you to say or ask such things as,

> Stan, how do you *feel* about this?

> Susan, our customer service staff is available whenever you want to *touch base.*

> Debbie, how does this *grab* you so far?

At the beginning of your sales presentation, you might ask a prospect,

What do you *feel* you'd like to accomplish as a result
of our meeting?

or,

What do you *feel* like accomplishing?

He'll know exactly how he feels about it because that's how kinesthetics think.
You'll be able to grab his emotions right out of his head. When you use kinesthetic predicates, a kinesthetic prospect will trust you because of how well you're
communicating with him.

When he is probing his prospect, one California life insurance salesman I
know often asks,

How do you *feel* about your job?
Do you *feel* like you'd like to provide for your family if something hap-
pened to you?
How would you *feel* if we got your premiums down?
How would you *feel* if you got sick and it was too late to do anything
about it?

These questions all work with the kinesthetic because they incorporate kinesthetic words.

You must also give a kinesthetic things to touch because if he can touch and
feel your ideas, he'll be sold five times faster.

If you are selling a personal computer with a mouse attachment, let him *hold*
the mouse and *feel* it glide along the tabletop. If you're selling typewriters, let
him *sit down* and use the keyboard. If you're selling fresh fruit and vegetables,
let your prospect hold them.

If your kinesthetic prospect can touch and feel the product, you'll sell more
than you thought possible, more than you've ever sold before. *You must be aware
of the cues he is sending you, both verbally and nonverbally.* So by all means, make
it easy for him to touch your product. If you do have a tangible product that
can be touched, be very aware that he may want to grasp it. When you see a
prospect reach out for a product—or even a sheet of paper—on which you're making notes or diagrams, suspect that he may be a kinesthetic and treat him like
one.

Even if your prospect turns out to be a visual, you can easily shift into the
visual mode. By paying attention to your prospect's reactions and words, you
really cannot make devastating mistakes. But if you treat a visual like a kinesthetic, he simply will not respond to you. Be aware of these things so you will
have the ability to change if you have to.

The Feel, Felt, Found Technique

Have you ever had the occasion to try to answer or counter your prospect's objections? (Another term for successfully countering your prospect's objections is "cashing," discussed in more depth in Chapter 15.) One great technique is to use a method called the *feel, felt, found technique.*

Here's how it works. The prospect might say to you,

> It's really too much money.

Your reply might be,

> I understand how you *feel.* Other prospects have *felt*
> the same way until they *found* out that. . . .

This is a great objection-handling technique for persuading people who operate in a kinesthetic mode.

But if your prospect is visual and says, "That's too expensive," and you use that technique, he is very likely to think you are being manipulative and superficial with him. Instead, he wants to hear visual predicates in your response to objections. To a visual you might combine visual words with the feel, felt, found technique and say,

> I *see* what you are talking about. Other clients of mine
> had the same *view* until they *found* out what the
> difference is between price and cost. Price is what you
> pay now. Cost is what you pay over a long period of
> time using my product.

How about auditories? What would you say to an auditory prospect?

> I *hear* what you are saying, Mr. Prospect. Other
> clients *told* me the same thing until they
> *found.* . . .

Not only must you use the right words, you must learn to fit them into the techniques and conversational patterns you are currently using when you answer objections, as well as in every other step of the sales process.

Remember that although people can react to visual, auditory, and kinesthetic cues, everyone has a primary mode in which they operate. Of course, no matter what our primary mode is, and no matter how uncomfortable it may be, we can shift into any mode we want. If you can become more flexible with your prospects and respond to them in their primary behavioral mode, however, you'll be able to build strong rapport and ultimately increase your sales and your profits.

CHAPTER 5

Building Rapport

Now that you've learned how to recognize and communicate with visuals, auditories, and kinesthetics, let's look at how you can use subliminal selling techniques to build rapport with them. In the remaining chapters, you'll learn a variety of techniques for examining the psychological underpinnings of rapport-building techniques.

Sharp salespeople know that if they can establish rapport with prospects, opportunities and favorable situations will present themselves. If you have poor rapport skills, however, people will avoid you like the plague. This is true in almost all of our relationships—from business to marriage to personal friendships. In this chapter, we look at how you can successfully and quickly establish rapport with your prospects.

What Is Rapport?

Rapport is simply a relationship marked by harmony, conformity, accord, or affinity. It helps the person you're communicating with find meaning and intent in the things you say. It helps him feel comfortable with you and creates a feeling of warmth and understanding.

When it comes to selling, rapport helps your prospect feel that what you're saying is aimed directly toward his particular needs and desires.

Without rapport, you're just communicating information; you might as well just *read* your sales presentation to the customer. If you can't establish rapport with your customer, chances are you won't make a sale.

You have to watch out for too much rapport as well, because if it's too high, you may end up doing more than just business: You may be taking your relationship out of the professional arena and into the personal or romantic realm.

Treating People the Way They Want to Be Treated

A million-dollar sales producer told me that when a client resists him, he knows rapport is too low. The resistance tells him that *he* is doing something wrong, not the client. It just means that of all the ways he has attempted to make contact and establish rapport, he hasn't yet found one single method that is useful with his client.

As communicators, we need to be flexible when we present ourselves to our clients. *Flexibility* includes the set of behavioral tools that we can use to more readily communicate and deal with our prospect or client.

You have learned in earlier chapters that visuals, auditories, and kinesthetics each want you to deal with them in a special way, to communicate with them through their own unique mode of communication.

If you are a visual you may communicate with such phrases as,

> Do you *see* what I mean?
>
> Does this *look* good to you?
>
> Is is *clear* so far?

If your prospect is not a visual, however, you will probably lose rapport and be even more likely to lose the sale.

But with high flexibility, you're able to deal with people the way they want to be dealt with. You're able to break the Golden Rule of treating people as you would have them treat you and instead treat people the way *they* want to be treated and communicate with them in the way *they* want.

The subliminal selling skills presented in this book allow you to reach a higher level of behavioral and sales flexibility, because you will recognize how your prospect wants to be sold and simply sell to him in his favorite way.

That flexibility will give you more alternatives and tools to use with your clients. You'll realize that if you are not getting the responses you want, you aren't treating people the way they want to be treated.

Techniques for Establishing Rapport

The best way to generate rapport is to genuinely and sincerely care about what your prospect needs or wants. No technique I can show you will work unless you really care about the person you are dealing with—and I can't show you how to care.

In this and the remaining chapters, you'll learn some verbal rapport techniques, such as *active listening,* and find out how to reinforce interpersonal trust and generate higher rapport by using small talk. You'll learn how to match voice quality, pace, pitch, and timbre, and you'll also learn about nonverbal rapport skills. You'll also be able to identify nonverbal clues and become adept at a technique called *nonverbal mirroring.*

But let's start by looking at some verbal strategies.

Active Listening

The most important goal of *active listening* is to get your prospect to sell himself on you and your product. Active listening may be the most important process in the sales cycle—more important than presenting your ideas, handling objections, or even closing—because if you learn what the prospect wants, what his needs are, and how his mind works as he communicates, you will be 100 percent certain of making a sale. If you give him exactly what he wants, there is no way he can say no to you.

Unfortunately, most of us don't listen. We keep talking and talking and talking to the point where we actually oversell. This really is a problem, since most of the time we sell right past the point of the prospect's buying. We start buying the product back.

This point was driven home to me when I spoke with a person who I hoped would hire me to help market his company's products. Since I'm a speaker and well-known in certain industries, I tried to persuade him that salespeople in those industries would come to hear me speak.

Since he was interested in selling his product, I suggested that he could get more people to hear about it if I was included in his seminar; attendance would increase and the loyalty of the attendees would increase toward his company; this would happen because few companies provide sales skills as a part of their product training. Obviously, the salespeople did not work for his company but were just brokers, acting like manufacturer's representatives.

As I stood there talking to him, I realized that I should shut up and let him talk to me.

When I probed him with questions, he raised some very serious objections. One was simply that my speaking fee was too high. He went on for almost a minute about how high-priced I was and how he couldn't afford my fee. I was very tempted to interrupt by telling him how much value he would receive by using me, but instead I kept quiet. By simply listening, I was astounded to hear him overcome his own objection as he said,

> But then again, I guess it would increase our
> corporate sales overall. I also think that these
> salespeople need information like this. It will
> increase our sales as well as their own production.
> Let's go ahead with it.

If I had interrupted him at any step during that interview process, I would have oversold. I would have bought back what I was trying to sell.

Here are several steps to help you effectively listen to your prospects and clients. These steps are so important that following them will literally make sales for you without your even trying to sell.

1. *Value the speaker.* Even though your prospect may not be as articulate as you, and you are sure you know what he is going to say anyway, you need to sincerely show that you value him for who he is.

2. *Develop the desire to hear the truth.* Your prospect may present objections or tell you things that you don't want to hear about your product or even about your sales abilities, but if you strive to hear the truth, you will avoid misunderstandings in the future.

In Proverbs 15:14, the Bible says:

> The wise man is hungry for the truth.

If you strive to be open to hearing the truth from your prospect instead of being locked into your own preconceived ideas, you will become a much better listener.

A manager of a very large company found that when members of his marketing staff received criticism, they were very quick to say, "Well he was just a crank anyway. What does he know? This person doesn't even pay his bills, why should we listen to him?"

That manager currently says to his marketing staff,

> Forget who said it; is there truth to it?
> Forget who's saying it. Listen for the truth.

3. *Make sure you take turns talking, and don't interrupt your prospect.* Research has shown that your prospect has an attention span of only thirty seconds at a time. Television advertisers have long known that if their advertisements last for more than thirty seconds, viewers will leave their set to get a cup of coffee or popcorn or even to go to the bathroom and that if a camera shot, even in a television program, is left in one place for more than 4.5 seconds, viewer interest will dissipate.

As a rule, make sure that you never again talk for more than thirty seconds without asking,

> Any comments on this? Any questions?

or asking for a response.

Thirty seconds really is a long time. Try timing yourself while talking; you'll be surprised by how long thirty seconds really is.

Marriage counselors know that when spouses have trouble communicating, it is because they frequently interrupt as soon as they hear something they don't like.

But remember: The thirty-second rule applies to you, the salesperson, not to the prospect. If you are very sharp, you will be able to control the interview more effectively by letting your prospect or client talk until he has communicated to his satisfaction, not yours.

Even though you would never ask your prospect out loud, "Well, are you through yet?" chances are you often think it. Realize that it's often more important for your prospect to hear himself tell you his problems than it is for you to hear them. If he thinks you are listening, he will be much more motivated to buy from you.

4. *Don't think about your response to your prospect while he is talking.* A good salesperson is sharp enough to be spontaneous, not canned, and he never tries to manipulate a prospect by asking certain questions whose answers he already knows.

Intensely listen to your prospect's answers before you speak; then answer in the way your prospect wants to hear it, if possible.

Thinking about what you want to say while the prospect is talking will certainly cause you to miss the message, and when you miss even the tiniest part of what your prospect is saying, you may be missing information that will generate a sale for you.

5. *Try to listen intensely so you can understand the situation from your prospect's point of view.* Your prospect has a point of view that is unique. You will not hear it from anyone else. You've never heard it before in quite the same way. Even though you may think you already understand his concerns, it is not actually what he says that's important, it's the process he goes through to say it.

Try to understand the thoughts behind your prospect's words. Remember, you are really dealing with perceptions, not just hard facts.

Listen to what he really thinks, not critically and analytically but as a window to the process he is going through. Say to yourself, "Well, that's what he believes."

A fool struggles to reveal constantly what is in his own mind, but a wise man struggles to understand not only what his prospect is saying but also what he is thinking.

6. *Show respect and consideration for every comment your prospect makes.* If your prospect realizes that you respect his words and value his comments, he will in turn respect you as somebody who can help solve his problems, not just peddle a product.

7. *Make sure that before you give your prospect an answer, you repeat his comments or concerns to show you understand.* In other words, verbalize what he says back to him. You just possibly may have heard something that the prospect didn't say or mean.

Here the concepts of *intent* and *meaning* come into play. If you can learn through better listening techniques what your prospect really means and present your message so that he understands the intent behind your words, you will make the sale.

8. *Maintain good eye contact.* Do not stare a prospect down, but keep a constant and natural communication through the eyes.

In Chapter 2, I mentioned that only visuals care about eye contact, seemingly gaining enormous amounts of information and determining honesty and whom to trust just by looking at the other person's pupils. While auditories and kinesthetics may not care deeply about eye contact, visuals certainly do. Remember the case of George Bush's and Geraldine Ferraro's great vice-presidential debates, where the viewing public thought that because Ferraro broke eye contact so much she might be hiding something?

In your case, don't take chances with any of your prospects. Maintain good eye contact, even if your prospect doesn't. Make sure that without staring your prospect down, you offer openness and honesty through constant and trusting eye contact.

9. *Don't take lots of notes while the prospect is speaking to you. Instead, jot down an occasional key word or phrase to help you recall the conversation later on.* I used to think that by keeping my ideas and views to myself too often, people would not be interested in me, but I've found that people care more about what they have to say than about what I think.

Letting the other person do the talking, particularly a sales prospect, is a key to greater sales. By repeating his own words back to him, you increase his feeling of importance and increase your level of rapport. When you begin to generate rapport with your client, the things you say are twice as meaningful to him.

There are three stages of selling to people:

1. During the first stage, you, the salesperson, are very new and try to talk people into doing the things you'd like them to do.
2. During the second stage, when you have more experience as a salesperson, you try to listen for openings and arguments and then try to talk people into doing what you'd like them to do.
3. By the third stage, when you are experienced and sharp in dealing with people, you let your client talk himself into doing the things you'd like him to do—simply because you are such a good listener.

When I spoke to a regional financial planning symposium, a bank management consulting company owner also spoke at the meeting. After his presentation, I had a cup of coffee with him.

I listened while he told me about his expertise in approaching banks and showing them how they could make more money by underwriting junk bonds (the funds with which corporations take over other companies). While he was talking, all I did was listen intensely and play back his favorite words constantly. During our ninety-minute conversation, I said almost nothing except when I wanted to reinforce some of his comments.

A month later he called me up and asked me to speak to the Young Presidents Organization, a group of men and women forty-nine years old and younger who are presidents of businesses with sales of over $10 million. When I asked why he picked me, he said he thought I was very wise and articulate and that many of the young presidents could learn a lot from me. This invitation was particularly curious to me, since he had found out almost nothing about me during our restaurant conversation. yet we had established good rapport because I had listened to him so actively. He had developed a strong bond with me simply because I had used the verbal playback strategy.

10. *Avoid certain habitual words and phrases that people use to generate superficial rapport.* Use of certain words and phrases is almost automatic in our society, but in fact, they generate very little rapport. For example:

> How are you?
> How's it going?

These are greetings that are particularly thoughtless in generating rapport.

For example, when was the last time someone told you how he felt just because you asked how he was? If someone has just cut her finger and you ask, "How are you?" she'll probably say, "Fine!" instead of saying, "I just cut my finger." If you ask somebody who's noticeably sick with the flu, "How are you?" he'll probably say, "Great, I'm fine!"

Or how about this? When you talk to somebody who's just been hurt in a baseball game and you ask, "Are you okay?" he'll almost always say, "I'm fine!"

What else would people say? It's a quick, impulsive, societal, automatic phrase that gets an automatic answer.

Reframing

Instead of using habitual words, try something called *reframing*. For example:

> Have your business meetings been going smoothly?

or,

> Has your day been productive?

or,

> Are things going smoothly for you?

Such reframing helps the person to think about what you just asked instead of passing the question off as meaningless.

The question shows that you are caring, and when you show you care, you'll establish more rapport.

Reframing is an act of changing the words that label a concept or idea. For example, simply by asking, "Has your day been productive?" you are forcing your prospect to think of her productivity that day. Using the phrase, "How are you?" basically asks the same thing, but your prospect has an automatic trigger response to the words:

> Fine.

She doesn't even think about it.

Insurance agents around the country have been trying to reframe their titles. Many have decided to put the words "Financial Services Adviser," or "Financial Consultant" on their business cards in an effort to avoid giving their prospects preconceived ideas about what an insurance agent is. The reframing seems to work, because the prospect's response often is:

> I don't need insurance. But I sure could use help with
> my finances as well as with my budgeting and
> investments.

Mary Kay Cosmetics has done a great job in reframing or relabeling its salespeople. Instead of simply calling its representatives cosmetic salespersons, this company calls them Mary Kay Consultants. The word "consultant" implies a professional who will help solve problems. In Mary Kay's case, these consultants help women look better and solve any cosmetic problems or improve appearance as best they can. They just also happen to be selling Mary Kay products.

Instant Replay Technique

Another strategy, which is discussed in greater detail in Chapter 12, is called *instant replay*.

The way people have previously bought in the past typically indicates how they will buy in the future, unless something traumatic has happened to change their typical buying patterns.

Do you believe that you can change any part of your personality if there is enough determination, motivation, and drive behind your desire? If you answered no, you're very close to the mark.

Even the smallest behavioral patterns are extremely difficult to change. Otherwise all marriages would be perfect the second time around. The problems are often not with the marriage partner but with you. Both parties must change.

Knowing this about people's ability to change will help you understand how your prospect will buy.

If you want to determine how someone will buy in the future, simply find out how he bought in the past. Here are some questions for you to try:

What made you decide to buy this product?
How did you decide to buy this?
Why did you buy this?

Here's what happened when one life insurance agent used this instant replay technique. She asked her prospect what had caused him to buy a certain policy some years before, and the prospect answered,

Because I needed more coverage for my family.

Since she knew that the prospect would probably still have the same concerns, the saleswoman appealed to the needs of his family, feeling confident that she was using an appropriate approach.

Let's say you're selling equity securities. The prospect might say,

I bought it because of track record.
I recognized the company name.
I wanted to see high growth.

If you play back those same concerns for the prospect's future, wouldn't you have a better chance of getting him to buy into your pitch? The funny thing is that if he says no to you after you've just replayed his past desires, in a sense he's denying himself.

Rapport-Building Words

There are certain key words that appeal to practically every American. Television, radio, and print advertisers use them with tremendous effectiveness. Some are so effective in drawing people in that companies even overuse them.

Have you ever read or heard the words, "new and improved?" Many Americans feel that if they see another "new and improved" label on a product, they'll throw it through a plate-glass window. Nonetheless, advertisers recognize that even these overused words continue to draw people to their product.

Do you ever use direct mail in your business? Effective and extremely tricky, direct mail can either make you a bundle or cost you a ton of money. Many companies have been able, through the use of great copy, to increase their direct mail response rates from an industry-accepted cold mailing standard of .5 percent all the way up to as much as 5 percent. These masters and experts of direct mail copy are simply using certain words to draw you in so that you'll read more of their ideas and remember more of what you see.

These same words can be used when you follow up with your prospect in writing. In fact, these words are so persuasive that they can also be used effectively in telephone conversations.

According to the October 1983 issue of *Life Notes*, published by the National Association of Life Underwriters (NALU), Yale University researchers have uncovered what they deem to be *the twelve most persuasive words to your prospect's ear*. These universal key words can make or break the rate of response you get:

1. *Discover.* Sears Financial Services rolled out its new credit card with the name "Discover." They put millions of dollars in trying to give American Express, Visa, and MasterCard a run for their money. Sears could not take a chance, but had to pick a name that research had deemed to be a word that generated positive interest.

2. *Easy.* Your prospects may have money, but what they want is more simplicity and ease in buying your products.

3. *Guarantee.* One of the fears most human beings have is taking risks. They want to know that if your product doesn't work, they can get their money back.

4. *Health.* It has often been said, "If I've got my health, I've got everything." To many people, health is even more important than money.

5. *Love.* Many companies make enormous amounts of money selling love. Whether its marketed through dating services or even singles' getaways, love is a big seller. Leo Buscaglia has become an international expert on what love is and how it should be shared. "Love" is definitely an emotion-laden word.

6. *Money.* Few people have enough, and everybody wants more.

7. *New.* "New" is simply a tried-and-true word that advertisers use to tap into the American mystique. If it's new, it must be better. Individuals who are selling products deemed old-fashioned have met with only moderate success. We look for things we have not seen before.

8. *Proven.* Most people want reliability. They want something that won't break down the first time they use it. They want it to work.

9. *Results.* As Americans, we don't care about best efforts. We don't care about trying hard. All we care about is winning. We want results. We want what we pay for to give us promised results.

10. *Safety.* Closely paralleling health, safety is valuable and important to people. If your product is safe, prospects are likely to trust it more.

11. *Save.* Saving money is almost as important as making money. Many advertisers in the media can't promise that you will make money, but they can help you save dollars you wouldn't have normally. Or more important, their product may even save you time.

12. *You.* With the onslaught of self-centered magazines such as *US* and *SELF*, the American public certainly wants to know that when you

advertise, you are not advertising to "us out there," but to "me." In other words, when you write copy or even a letter, use the word "you." It has a magnetic way of drawing your reader or listener in so that you are not overgeneralizing in your approach.

Matching Voice, Timbre, Pitch, and Pace

Establishing rapport increases the rate at which a prospect trusts and respects your ability to get a job done. You'll also want to match a prospect's voice timbre, pitch, and pace and even the quality of his vocabulary and articulation.

Timbre, pitch, and pace refer to how your voice sounds. *Timbre* is the resonance of your voice. In all three of the *Star Wars* movies, George Lucas wanted a very masterful, domineering, and aggressively evil warrior. He not only made Darth Vader look evil but he used James Earl Jones, whose voice was so resonant that he even sounded evil. This is not to say that timbre is evil, but it is what makes your voice project.

Pitch is how high or low your voice is. You can sound like a parakeet or as low as a tuba playing a John Philip Sousa march.

Pace is the speed of your voice. You probably have a slow or fast vocal pattern, and this is not likely to change. Most people speak at somewhere around 125 words a minute, although that depends somewhat on where you live in the United States.

About a year into my speaking career, I spoke in Birmingham, Alabama. I was thirty minutes into my hour-long program when a man in the back row raised his hand. I didn't want to get off track because I had a limited amount of time, so I ignored the guy. Unfortunately, he kept his hand raised for about ten straight minutes, which started to distract people around him. I finally recognized him and asked if he had a question. He sat back in his chair, put his thumbs in his belt, and said in a very loud Southern drawl,

> Son, I'd like to know what you said after you said "hello."

Obviously I was speaking too fast and had developed very little rapport. If I had thought I was getting the message across to him or to any other people in the room, I had been sadly mistaken. I was wasting my time and theirs.

One of the best ways to establish verbal rapport is to listen intensely to your prospect for the first three or four minutes and mentally record everything you hear. Listen to his word-inflection patterns, the length of his sentences, even how he marks out key words. This information will help you sell him subliminally by duplicating his voice pattern.

People who make their living by telemarketing have to be masterful in matching key words and phrases. The way they say things is crucially important because the person on the other end of the telephone has nothing else to go on.

A secretary I know in northern Florida used to feel nervous, almost to the point of panic, when she had to speak to New Yorkers. She found, however, that when she quickened her normal Florida drawl, used some New York slang, and added a slight New York staccato to her speech, she actually got more business for her boss.

When I speak to people from the South on the telephone, I often use the phrase "you all" and add a bit of Southern drawl to my voice. The funny thing is, they rarely ever comment about my accent.

People actually expect you to talk the way they do. When you don't communicate in their normal style or you mismatch, you're the one who's causing tension, not them.

When I spoke to a group in Lake Charles, Louisiana, the audience was comprised of salespeople who were mostly Southerners with marked Southern accents. They had a very slow style of speaking and very down-home attitudes. The other speaker on the platform, who was from southern California as I was, spoke much too fast for this audience. I suppose he had no idea of the mismatching that was going on or of the low rapport and trust between him and his audience.

I, on the other hand, had prepared for this program by listening intensely to how these Southerners spoke so that I could get an idea of the pace and pitch of their speech and the words they used to express themselves. I purposely matched them as I addressed the audience, in order to gain as much rapport as possible.

Once you've established rapport, there are some very interesting ways you can make use of it to persuade your prospects to commit themselves to your ideas. In Chapters 6 through 14, I'll discuss several methods you can use to maintain rapport and sell to your prospects.

CHAPTER 6

Matching or Mirroring

One of the best ways to generate rapport and trust is to use a technique called *matching* or *mirroring*. Simply stated, the technique involves matching the prospect's key words, phrases, and actions.

Identifying and Matching Key Words and Phrases

Even though there are more than 300,000 words in the dictionary, most people use only about one percent of them. People also have a subset of those words that hold special meanings for them.

If you can identify and use those keys words and phrases, you will be able to unlock your prospects' minds.

Adults develop key words or slang. I'm sure you've heard these expressions:

It was really a rip-off.

Laid-back.

Tough.

A piece of cake.

He was a tiger.

Most people, when they use selective words, pause just before and just after using them. This is called *marking out*. For example, one realtor I know listens very hard when a prospect describes what he wants in a property. For example, if after talking for a few minutes, her prospect says,

What I want is an [*pause*] incredible [*pause*] view.

then, when she shows a house with the kind of view he wants, she reinforces the idea by *marking out* the same key word that the prospect had used initially:

Tom, here's that house you were talking about.
And I think you'll agree with me that you are looking
right now at an [*pause*] incredible [*pause*] view.

Notice she doesn't just say a "good" view. She uses words with a special meaning for her prospect. In this way, she grabs his emotions rather than just conveying information. She gets him to think in terms of what he really wants, rather than what she thinks he wants.

It's important also to note that when the realtor hears a word such as "incredible" marked out, she asks on the spot what it means to the prospect—an incredible view to one person could mean the city skyline; to another, tall trees; to somebody else, it could mean an unobstructed view of the neighborhood.

A life insurance agent told me a story about a meeting he had had with a prospect. He had used my ideas to understand his prospect's vocabulary, especially key words and phrases. He listened intensely while probing. His job was to uncover his prospect's financial needs, and he heard the prospect say that she wanted protection with an increase in income as an investment.

These were not the words that the agent had learned to associate with the products he sold. He was accustomed to saying "security with income protection." He decided, however, to try my suggestion and use the woman's own key words, so he said,

I understand that you want *protection* with an *increase*
in *income*. Here's how this product will help you. . . .

You see? He reused the words that were meaningful to her. He didn't try to change her way of describing what she wanted. Instead, being flexible, he adapted to and matched the words that she was already comfortable with.

During those first few minutes with your prospect, it's crucial that you listen to the way he says things. When you play back words and phrases that hold extra meaning for him, you're bound to establish rapport and increase your sales.

Key phrases are used by everyone. Everyone has their own set of experiences that contribute to who they have become. These experiences are readily heard and observed from how they communicate.

For example, Jimmy Carter used to use the term "turn the corner." Every time he tried to explain his policies to the American public, he would say, "turn the corner." In one of his speeches he said,

> We have just turned the corner on inflation.

Then he said,

> We have just turned the corner on the deficit.

Then he said,

> We have just turned the corner on unemployment.

And last, he said,

> We have just turned the corner on oil prices.

When I heard that, I couldn't help but think that the country had turned four corners and was back where it had started.

If you listen closely to your prospects' phrases, you will be able to communicate with them in the way they want. Make sure to carry a pen and paper with you so you can write down these key phrases as they talk. Then when the time comes, you can *match* their own words and phrases when presenting and closing. Use these words and phrases back on your prospects at every opportunity.

I once called a vice-president of a stock brokerage firm on a referral. I listened well and talked with him for about twenty minutes. As he said goodbye, he signed off with this phrase: "Whatever you do, Kerry, do it well, have fun, and do plenty of it."

Guess how I signed off on a letter that I later sent to him? By *mirroring* his key phrase, even in a letter, I picked up one of the easiest sales I ever made.

Nonverbal Mirroring

Nonverbal matching and mirroring can be used as a nonverbal method of establishing rapport. People tend to do business with or put their trust in people who are most like them. If you are dissimilar or too unlike your prospect, it will take longer to build the warmth, trust, and rapport necessary to make a sale.

One of the ways you can promote trust and rapport is to mirror body movement and posture. Let me give you an example:

When I spoke at a sales conference in northern California, I had breakfast the morning before my presentation with another speaker on the program. While we had our coffee, I didn't say a single word. I just listened to him talk, and mirrored his body movements.

I crossed my arms when he crossed his. I crossed my legs when he crossed his. When he leaned forward, I leaned forward, and so on. He said he enjoyed my company so much and felt we had developed such good rapport that he asked me to speak to his company on communication skills. He had no idea that I had simply been mirroring all of his movements to create the rapport he enjoyed so much.

Mirroring or matching body movements is really a by-product of having incredibly high rapport. You see it in friends, but not in enemies. Adversaries will deliberately, although often unconsciously, mismatch. If one adversary crosses his legs, the other person will uncross his. If one has her hands on her hips, the other will put hers at her side. In fact, adversaries will often break eye contact rather than allow rapport to be created.

You often see this in husbands and wives who are not getting along. If husbands and wives watched their movements more often, they would create what is called a *romantic dance.* It's hard not to be in high rapport when you're sitting alike and moving alike. It helps to promote thinking alike.

Have you ever noticed that your friends frequently cross their arms the same way you do when sitting with you? When you are talking together, they lean toward you in what is called *choral unison.* From videotaped studies, you can see that when people are in unison or thinking alike, they typically mirror not only body language but also voice, pace, and speed. They're actually trying to be more like each other in an effort to cut down verbal, physical, and behavioral differences between them.

The bottom line is that if you can mirror your prospect and imitate his posture and physical movements, you are going to generate high rapport. Along with rapport comes trust, and when you gain trust, you get business.

You can tell that you have established rapport and trust with your prospect by the way he matches your movements. If you say something he doesn't like, however, mismatching will often occur and the mirroring will stop. These signals are extremely useful in helping you to determine what he does and does not like about your presentation—the things you say and do in his presence.

Once you've noticed what your prospect looks like when he's interested, you have done something called *calibration*. You literally have determined his own set of unique nonverbal cues to let you know what he is thinking. For example, if you have noticed that he leans forward when he's interested and happy, what do you do you surmise when he leans back? He could be showing you negativity or even defensiveness. When you become really good at recognizing your prospect's thought modes by his overt, unique nonverbal cues, you will be much more aware of what to say to him and what he responds to best. You will literally cut down your sales cycle and increase trust.

If you see your prospect breaking rapport suddenly, this is an obvious sign that you're heading in the wrong direction. Don't make things difficult for yourself. Change your strategy instead.

Crossover Mirroring

Crossover mirroring is imitating a prospect's nonverbal gesture with a different part of the body.

A salesman once wrote me that he was nervous about mirroring the exact nonverbal gestures of his prospects. He was concerned that prospects might think he was mocking or making fun of them. I suggested he use *crossover mirroring*.

If your prospect crosses his arms, then you cross your legs. If your prospect's head is resting on his hand, then you might touch your chin. If your prospect's hands are in his pockets, then you fold your hands in your lap very close to your pockets. These crossover mirroring techniques are enormously effective and will increase rapport very quickly. And rapport, as you know by now, is your ticket to greater profits.

Obviously, matching or mirroring a client or prospect should not be overdone; you should not mimic your prospect. But done subtly, matching and mirroring can help to build or maintain rapport with a prospect.

A good example of subtle, yet effective, matching and mirroring can be seen in the case of a consulting psychologist who was called upon by a realtor to help her negotiate a fee due her by a past employer. Apparently, the realtor had sold a few properties and had earned a $10,000 commission, which her employer was unwilling to pay. To further complicate matters, there was some discrepancy over the actual commission that had been negotiated thus far.

The psychologist attended the meeting between the realtor and the broker. Immediately the broker looked at the psychologist and asked, "What is she doing here?"

The realtor responded, "Oh, she's just a consultant I decided to bring in."

The broker responded, "This is between you and me. She can stay as long as she doesn't say a word."

During the entire negotiation the consultant mirrored and matched body posture with the broker. When the broker crossed his legs, she crossed her arms. When he leaned forward, she leaned forward. After about forty minutes, the broker conceded and agreed to pay the realtor $10,000, exactly the amount of money the realtor was hoping to get.

During the entire confrontation, every time the broker said something positive or conciliatory to the realtor, the consultant would come close to matching his posture. Every time the broker said something negative or counterproductive, the consultant would mismatch his posture. The funny thing was that at the end of the meeting, the broker commented to the consultant, "It's too bad you had to sit silently through all of this."

The broker had had no idea of the consultant's enormous power over him simply because she had matched and mismatched his movements.

Rapport is like money. With it you will find opportunity everywhere. Without it, you will soon go broke. Rapport is crucial to establishing good working relationships with your clients. Its most important role is as a checking system—to make sure the communication process you are using with your prospects is working.

CHAPTER 7

Leading and Pacing

In long-distance cross-country races there is usually a man or woman who sets the pace for that race. The pacer is not always a person expected to win but rather, a person the other runners try to keep up with. The rest of the runners try to stay neck and neck with the pacer in an effort to keep him from winning the race.

As a subliminal selling skill technique, pacing means moving all of your behavioral makeup to fit your prospect. Whether it's voice mode, nonverbal cues, or phrases, when you pace a prospect, you are trying to be as close to him mentally as possible.

Leading is somewhat different. When a marathon runner suddenly puts on the steam, he takes the lead. It's up to the others to match his lead by trying to keep up with him.

You too can lead and pace a client to the behavior or reactions you desire when you have established good rapport with him.

To understand how leading and pacing work, imagine a flock of geese flying together in formation. Notice that if the lead goose deviates and flies a little to the left, the rest of the geese don't go right or straight ahead but follow in tight formation right behind that lead goose.

The Basics of Leading

Here's how to lead:

1. *Make sure to duplicate whatever posture your prospect takes during your meeting with him.* If the prospect crosses her legs, you cross yours. If she puts one hand over the back of the sofa, you do the same.

2. *Establish nonverbal rapport very quickly.* When you sincerely feel that rapport is becoming deeper and deeper, generate more enthusiasm and higher attention in your prospect by slowly leaning forward. Uncross your legs. Put your forearms on your thighs. You'll find that *you will generate enthusiasm by leaning forward,* and your client will probably lean forward too. If she doesn't lean forward and follow your lead, retreat. Then start from ground zero.

The Mechanics of Pacing and Leading

The evening before I spoke before a meeting of the Texas Jaycees, the president of that group asked all of the speakers to get together to discuss the next day's presentations. At that get-together I got into a conversation with Tom, the director of the National Jaycee organization.

As Tom and I sat and talked, I paced him by *mirroring* his behavior. I crossed my legs in exactly the way he crossed his. I made sure that my arms rested on the chair in the same fashion his did. I found we were developing a very high level of rapport and trust.

Then I noticed something very interesting: When I smiled, he smiled. When I decided to uncross my legs, he did the same thing within ten or fifteen seconds. He uncrossed his legs and mirrored me instead of my mirroring him. I was now able to lead Tom rather than pace him. You can determine if you have high rapport with a prospect when he begins to follow your lead.

Million-dollar sales producers establish such high rapport with their prospects that they are able to be very effective persuaders. They pace and lead their prospects. They sit the same way the prospect sits. They move the same way the prospect moves. Then, after a very short amount of time, the prospect starts moving in their direction, toward their line of thought both verbally and nonverbally.

Have you ever been in a discussion with somebody who had a radically different point of view from you yet presented an argument so persuasively that you felt yourself agreeing? Your reaction was the result of a complex process, but it probably started with his mirroring your hands, head, feet, and even head-tilt. He also probably tried to agree with you on most of the things you talked about before he tried to lead you to his opinion. When we have rapport, we struggle to maintain it. When rapport is broken, it often causes psychological discomfort.

In the middle of a meeting with a financial planner I was visiting in Appleton, Wisconsin, I noticed that his client was sitting all the way back in his chair. The planner, whose name was Frank, stayed back in the same position. After about two or three minutes, Frank sensed that he had established high rapport. Then, he suddenly leaned forward and started talking about the goals he wanted to accomplish in that meeting. His client also leaned forward. Because of the rapport Frank had built with his client, he was able to lead him.

Closing the sale at that point was almost a shoo-in. Frank knew that if he could lead his prospect to sit forward, the prospect would feel the same enthusiasm Frank had for achieving his goals.

The natural question is: Did the prospect sit forward because he was enthusiastic, or did enthusiasm follow when he sat forward? Frank believed that if he could lead his prospect into sitting forward, the action would affect his behavior by increasing his enthusiasm.

Pacing and Leading Large Groups

Good public speakers, especially motivational speakers, can even use the techniques of pacing and leading with large groups of people. They will match and mirror such elements of the group's behavior as body posture for a few minutes and then lead the group to do what they want them to do.

I recently had the opportunity to watch a motivational speaker at work. As he was introduced, there was a round of applause for him, but the audience had settled back in their chairs with their arms crossed, looking fairly unenthusiastic.

The speaker crossed his arms at the podium and spoke fairly quietly, trying to match and mirror the group. He even put his hands in his pockets. Here he was using the technique of *crossover mirroring* discussed in Chapter 6.

But, as the presentation progressed, he began to use his hands a little bit more to illustrate ideas. He modulated his voice and gradually grew more excited and enthusiastic. He even matched and mirrored the group verbally. Not surprisingly, the audience began to follow his lead, and their enthusiasm followed his.

Pacing worked for him because of the group's lack of enthusiasm. When people have low levels of motivation and enthusiasm, they typically do not talk with very much excitement. If this speaker had come on strong and been a motivated fireball, it is very likely that he would have lost rapport. But since he had started out with (assumed) low motivation and low levels of enthusiasm, he was able to mirror the audience's general attitude, slowly becoming more enthusiastic and more excited, which caused the audience to follow his emotional lead.

The technique this motivational speaker used to mirror his audience nonverbally is a fairly complex one. Have you ever noticed that most audiences contain groupings of people who typically have high rapport and mirror each other? Very successful and experienced speakers know that most audiences consist of such groupings who know each other and because of proximity find out a little about each other. This familiarity causes them to also mirror each other's body language. So when these experienced speakers mirror a large audience they don't mirror every single attendee, they mirror groups.

For example, if one group of people sits with arms crossed, a speaker may cross his when he makes eye contact with that group. When he sees another group of people sitting forward, if he is a good speaker, he leans forward too as he talks to them. This is very effective, because a good speaker does not talk to just one part of an audience; he talks to groups of attendees and audiences as he makes and breaks eye contact.

A speaker is able to pace a group verbally by saying things that match what the audience is already thinking:

> You've come here today to get some great ideas, and
> you're very bright people, so you probably know that
> this idea is one of the best ideas you'll ever hear.

He gears or paces the group by telling people what they already know: (1) that they have come here today and (2) that they are bright people. Then he leads them to his own ideas, namely, that they are hearing one of the best ideas ever. In this way, he leads them into thinking what he wants them to think.

Why Pacing Works

In most cases, people struggle to gain and maintain rapport with one another. When a person leads us, we unconsciously realize that rapport could be broken if we were left behind. So we pace the person by staying up with him.

You have probably been paced by salespeople in stores. If you have high self-esteem, you probably think of yourself as fairly intelligent, good-looking, fun to be with, enjoyable, trustworthy, and honest. When someone tells you these things in a conversation, even though he is telling you what you already know, he is actually pacing your thought patterns. He is communicating with you and moving along the highway you're already on.

One of the ways people get us to agree with them on controversial subjects such as politics and religion is through pacing and leading. They first make a series of statements that nobody can disagree with, such as:

> I know you care about your country and the freedoms we
> all share.

Then they present their unique philosophy or viewpoint. Some followers find themselves agreeing with that particular philosophy because their rapport with the speaker is so high that they feel unable to break that rapport.

On a piece of direct mail I received for a seminar, the cover said:

> You are reading this flyer.
> You are looking at the words.
> You are thinking: Is it worth it?
> You will get ideas to help you increase your sales by 100 percent
> in the next three weeks.

The flyer was designed to pace the reader by making undeniably true statements such as, "You are reading this flyer; you are looking at the words" and leading him to a new line of thought once he has attained a moderate level of rapport with the written copy.

Sincerity: The Key to Pacing

Of course, some salespeople will use pacing insincerely, and I'm not suggesting that you do that. Some people use pacing techniques like this in telephone prospecting:

> Mr. Prospect, you're a very bright man. You understand
> life. You understand economics. That's why you'll buy
> this 29-inch television for $699 because you realize
> this is such a good deal.

But the prospect says,

> No, I don't realize this is such a good deal. But I'm
> going to give you three orders anyway: Hang up, don't
> call back, and leave me alone.

The key to using proper pacing is simple. Just make sure that you're sincere in your statements. Then it's easy to make undeniably true statements that the listener really believes and agrees with.

When I was scheduled to be the keynote speaker at one of the biggest sales conventions in the world, I had a lousy time slot on the program. I was to speak in the afternoon. Every speaker wants to get an audience in the morning before they've had to listen to a lot of speakers and be fatigued by a big lunch. When I called the program chairman, I realized that I would have a very difficult time getting him to change my speaking time. So I said,

> John, it's good to talk to you. I've been looking   *
> forward to speaking to your convention for a long time.
> I'm excited because it is the biggest conference in the
> world within its industry. You all have a reputation
> for running possibly the best convention of its kind
> anywhere. I'm sure that you also want to make sure that
> the attendees are ready to hear the right speaker at
> the right time. That's why I would like to be the first
> speaker in the morning. I think that with my kind of
> presentation, they'll be more uplifted and excited for
> the rest of the speakers during the day.

I had paced John by sincerely complimenting him on how wonderful I thought his group was as well as on the organization of the meeting. I had also appealed to his already well-developed sense of timing the right speaker in the right place. After I had developed rapport with him by pacing things he already knew and felt good about, I led him into believing that the attendees would be better-served by using me as the first speaker, in the morning rather than in the afternoon.

I was rescheduled as the morning speaker.

Rapport: Know How to Get It and When You Have It

Now that you know something about verbal and nonverbal pacing and leading, wouldn't you like to see for yourself how easy it is to use these techniques once you've established rapport?

Try this experiment in a restaurant: Pick out a table from which the person sitting at it has a view of you, or is at least facing in your direction. After a few minutes, begin to physically mirror that individual. If he has his head in his hands, put your head in your hands. If he crosses his legs with the right leg over the left, you do the same. If his head is cocked to one side, mirror that.

Then, after a few minutes of mirroring, change something: Try moving your head in the opposite direction; take your head out of your hands; put your feet flat on the floor without crossing your legs. If you have done a good job of pacing, mirroring, and establishing rapport, the person sitting at a different table will probably follow your lead and mirror your physical actions.

Think of how effective this can be for you in a sales situation. You can actually change your prospect's comfort level by first gaining rapport and then leading him in the mental direction you want him to go.

Leading works because, once there is rapport, your prospect will struggle to maintain that rapport. You know rapport is high when your prospect mirrors you both verbally and nonverbally. You are able to lead his attitudes and perceptions simply because you have generated rapport that is so high that your prospect is terribly uncomfortable with breaking it, so uncomfortable, in fact, that he would rather be led by you than break rapport and keep his own point of view.

A man from Knoxville, Tennessee, Art Abboud, described one of the best cases of pacing and leading I've ever heard. Have you ever had a prospect who was negative, disinterested, or who didn't want to spend time with you? Well, Art experienced this with a prospect.

The prospect was thirty minutes late to an appointment he had set up in his own office. Art waited patiently. Finally, the prospect walked into his own office, saw Art sitting in the reception area, and came up to him with his arms crossed:

PROSPECT: Art, I can't see you this morning, I'm too busy.
ART [*standing up, recognizing the prospect's arms are crossed, and crossing his own arms in turn*]: When would you like to reschedule this?
PROSPECT [*looking at John's crossed arms*]: How long will this take if I see you right now?
ART: Ten minutes, unless you ask me questions.
PROSPECT: Well, if that's all it will take, I'll talk to you right now rather than reschedule.

They both walked into the prospect's office, whereupon the prospect sat in his chair and Art sat in the chair opposite him. The prospect, disinterested, crossed his arms and legs.

PROSPECT: You have ten minutes. So, what have you got?

Art started talking, but simultaneously crossed his legs and arms just as his prospect did.

After four or five minutes, the prospect became even more negative and crossed his legs even tighter. But when he interlocked his fingers behind his head and leaned back in the high wing chair, guess what Art did?

He crossed his legs and interlocked his fingers behind his head.

Art then did something seemingly stupid, but it turned out to be the best thing he could have done at this meeting: He broke rapport by leaning forward in his chair and placing his arms on the prospect's desk. Breaking rapport is normally a foolhardy thing to do, but the prospect, in an effort to preserve rapport, also leaned forward and placed his hands on his desk. Art then looked him straight in the eye:

ART: You're going on vacation next week, let's get this taken care of right now before you leave.

PROSPECT [*smiling*]:   Great, let's do it.

In order to get the prospect to buy, Art had to know as much about people skills as he did about his product. In fact, Art knew so much about his prospect that in order for the prospect to say no to Art, he would have first had to say no to himself.

Pacing and Leading With Verbal Cues

Pacing and leading work not only with body language and nonverbal techniques but also with verbal cues. I spent a week in Tennessee where I spoke at association conferences at five of the biggest cities in that state. When I came back to California, my wife told me that I sounded like someone from the backwoods of the Smokey Mountains. Without realizing it, I had tried so hard to stay in rapport with those friendly Tennesseeans that I had actually let them lead me to talk the way they talked, with the same voice inflection, speed, and pitch.

You can do the same thing with people you know whom you would like to change. For example, if you talk to a prospect from the South on the telephone, first try to speak as slowly as he does to generate rapport. Then speed up gradually to a level quicker than his initial speed. Ultimately you will find that he will talk as quickly as you do to preserve rapport.

Closing Difficult Prospects

An insurance salesman wrote me about how he had used a physical pacing and leading technique on a business owner who was very difficult to communicate with. The businessman would always sit with his legs and arms crossed during their conversations and his presentations, and the salesman couldn't make any progess.

At their next meeting, the salesman used my ideas of matching and mirroring the business owner and paced him during the first twenty minutes. After the twenty minutes had passed and rapport was fairly high, he leaned forward, hoping to lead his prospect into greater enthusiasm and excitement about his ideas.

The business owner, whom the salesman had found so difficult to even get to talk before, now displayed trust and rapport. He leaned over when my friend did, nodded his head in agreement when the salesman did, showed very high levels of rapport, and stayed that way. My friend wrote to me and said,

> Kerry, I couldn't believe what happened. All I know is that I closed him. The man wrote me a check for $25,000, $12,000 of which was my commission for the day. Kerry, I wish I'd used your techniques fifteen years earlier. I could have made ten times the amount of money I've made up to now.

CHAPTER 8

Anchoring

One of the most effective ways to give hidden commands to your prospects is to *anchor* them. Anchoring is the technique of eliciting memories and emotions in people by using verbal or nonverbal cues. Using anchoring, you can subliminally change someone's attitude.

The term "anchoring" derives from an obvious source. When a ship drops its anchor, it does so to hold it firmly in place. When you anchor someone, you are holding him in place by using words or actions that make him feel comfortable in your presence. If he associates particular words or actions with positive feelings, once you discover what those words or actions are, you can anchor your prospect into feeling with a similar positive attitude.

Anchor in the Prospect's Primary Mode

Some of the most elegant communicators and salespeople in the world will anchor by using the prospect's predominant thinking mode—visual, auditory, or kinesthetic. If the prospect is a visual, he'll use visual anchors. If the prospect is auditory or kinesthetic, he will anchor sounds or feelings.

A visual prospect will respond better to things he can see, view, or picture. Once you've established high rapport with a visual, you can use visual anchors such as smiling, pointing a finger in the air, or nodding your head. To close a sale with a visual prospect, you can control his emotions by associating that same gesture with your attempt to sell.

When I give a speech, I will visually anchor laughter. I'll tell a joke or a funny story and broadly smile to initiate an anchor. Then later, when I'd like the group to laugh or chuckle at a particular time, I'll smile broadly again. The group will laugh more readily. I've anchored them. They know when I smile it's their cue to laugh.

An auditory responds to things he can hear, such as pace, pitch, and sounds. Good anchors for an auditory would be snapping fingers, clapping hands, tapping objects, or changing voice inflection. He'd even respond to something as simple as a change in the pitch of your voice.

When you are ready to anchor an emotion with an auditory, make your voice go very high at the end of a question:

Isn't this a [*raise pitch of voice*] great idea?

Then when you are ready to close, use the same inflection in your voice. This reestablishes the emotions your prospect felt when you anchored him initially. Using individualized anchoring techniques like this, you'll increase your profits by at least 25 percent.

Kinesthetics are probably the easiest people to anchor because they respond to touch. They are swayed through emotional or gut responses. If you can touch them with a pencil or with your hand, you will anchor the emotion they were feeling at the time you touched them. For example, if you tell a joke or are using your sense of humor, simultaneously touch the person as you tell the punch line, anchoring the emotion they felt as you were telling the joke. Then, as you are closing, touch them again to bring back the same good emotion you anchored before.

Creating Anchoring Cues

You can create your own set of cues tailored to your particular prospects. You can create nonverbal messages and influence your prospect by having him associate even a single word with the cues that have become his anchors.

I was at a sales meeting having a conversation with a manager. As we were developing rapport, I kept the discussion on tennis, golf, and airline travel, and when I felt that our rapport was at its highest possible point, I touched him on the arm. After about forty minutes, I presented my ideas on sales training and tried to close the sale. Again I touched him on the arm, in the same place as before. He went for my ideas as if they were his own.

Touching his arm elicited the same feelings of high rapport we'd had when I had touched him earlier in the conversation.

The best time to create an anchor is when rapport is at its peak. You can use touch, as I did, or you can smile, point a finger, raise your eyebrows, or snap your fingers—many nonverbal gestures will work to associate a moment of trust. Then you will be able to recreate that trust or high rapport instantly by using the same gesture.

Here's another example. A friend of mine who is a financial planner recently told me that in the middle of a conversation he had asked his client,

> What is the most important aspect of tax shelters according to
> your philosophy?

The client replied,

> Well, I guess security is the most important thing to me. I don't like
> to take risks.

My friend repeated the prospect's desire for a shelter with low risk, but as he did so he raised his eyebrows. In other words, he anchored his prospect visually.

During his presentation about some mutual funds, he had an idea that he felt was just right for his client. The planner said,

> Mr. Prospect, this fund will give you not only high
> growth, it's a tax shelter with low risk.

Just when my friend said "low risk," he raised his eyebrows. He said he could literally see his prospect's eyes light up. The prospect smiled and said,

> That sounds great to me. Let's go ahead with it right
> now.

If you really want to instill commitment in your buyers, you can literally control their emotions and actually change their response level through anchoring. It's simple to do. The most important point is to try it yourself.

Stealing Anchors

People possess their own unique and personal anchors. You'll find that most of them have their own nonverbal communication methods and techniques with special meanings that are exclusively theirs. Just imagine how effective you could be if you could steal someone's personal anchors. You wouldn't have to create new ones if you could find out what your prospect's particular anchors meant to him.

Everyone has certain gestures that hold personal meaning for him. When you find out what those gestures and meanings are, you can use them on your prospect. This is a truly personal form of anchoring.

When I spoke before a financial corporation in Cincinnati, I noticed that the vice-president of marketing had an interesting way of shaking his head horizontally from side to side, as if thinking no when actually he meant yes.

It was a strange, nonverbal gesture. Even when we talked face-to-face, I noticed that when he thought yes, he shook his head from side to side. In presenting the idea of doing sales training for his managers, I actually stole his anchor.

When I wanted him to commit to the idea, I shook my head horizontally from side to side. I was fascinated to watch his facial expression immediately change to understanding and excitement and to hear him say, "It sounds like a good idea to me. Let's start right away."

The best way to steal anchors is to watch your prospect for four or five minutes to discover what his unique anchors are. Then you are free to use them back on the prospect.

It is really very easy to do. Try it a couple of times to test it. If you experiment with your prospect and he responds, you've got it. If he doesn't respond, you've probably just used the wrong anchor. Try another one on him. He'll be entirely unaware of what you are doing.

Chances are it will make a winner out of you in almost any sales situation.

CHAPTER 9

Hidden Commands

Some phrases seem to generate specific responses from people. We refer to these as *hidden commands* or *trigger words*. They essentially function as an oral version of anchoring. These phrases can help maintain rapport and get prospects to think the way you'd like them to think.

A major research effort conducted by social psychologist Ellen J. Langer of Harvard University* studied the effect trigger words have for people. Langer discusses what happened when a number of university students were in line to photocopy some documents:

First, the researcher walked to the front of the line and said,

> I need to make this copy fast; do you mind?

Then a (researcher) student walked to the front of the line and said,

> I need to make this copy fast *because* my car is double
> parked. Do you mind?

---

*Robert Cialdini, "The Triggers of Influence." *Psychology Today*, February 1984, 43–44.

Can you guess which researcher had the most success?

Langer determined from this that a student using the key word "because" was three times more likely to gain access to the front of the copy machine line as one not using the word.

Now you might be thinking that the word "because" was not as much of a catalyst as the double-parked car. But another study tested this very hypothesis: The researcher walked to the front of the line and said,

> I need to make this copy fast; my car is double parked
> and I need to go.

But he didn't use the word "because." Even in this case, the researcher was not allowed to cut in line nearly as often as the researcher who simply used the word "because."

The word "because" acted as a trigger to cause the people in line to allow the student to cut to the front.

Autosuggestion

One of the great sales superstars in the insurance business uses some seemingly hypnotic techniques on his prospects, techniques that fall into the category of *autosuggestion*. He might say,

> I found that a million-dollar policy was the best way
> to go for another client of mine whose circumstances
> were quite similar to yours. Do you see what I'm
> saying, Justin?

emphasizing the words, "million dollar policy was the best way to go." He gives an honest, but suggestive, command that the prospect can't help but receive, reinforcing the idea that it is the right thing to do at the right time.

Underlining Messages

The concept of giving hidden commands revolves around underlining certain parts of your ideas. If you're like me, I'm sure you find that your prospects don't remember things you'd like them to remember. Instead, they focus on certain ideas, which they remember better than others.

I want to help my prospects remember things I'd like them to retain. I want to give them hidden messages inside the words I speak to help them focus on certain product benefits or ideas I think they will respond to better. That's why using a phrase such as,

John, this will work for you,

is effective if "work for you" is emphasized.

Using the
Client's Own Words

One of the most effective things you can do is to turn your prospects' favorite phrase into a hidden command.

One of my prospects worked with a large medical corporation in California. Whenever he talked about the corporate officers, her referred to them as "those people in the puzzle palace." Because he used the term so frequently, I knew it was something that had meaning for him. All I did was turn the phrase into a hidden command, and I was able to sell him by saying,

Jim, I especially think those people in the *puzzle palace* are going to enjoy this.

I marked out, emphasized, and effectively made a hidden command out of the phrase, "those people in the puzzle palace," If they would enjoy it, Jim would also enjoy it.

Using Positive Hidden Commands

Hidden commands can reinforce potential behavior and help the prospect come to a decision faster. But your prospect probably won't respond if you use a negative hidden command—such as suggesting that the prospect would be blowing the opportunity of a lifetime by not investing in your product.

Avoid presenting negative reasons for doing something. Instead, use positive ideas such as,

John, a municipal bond mutual fund right now is a good idea

Hidden Command Words

Some words you may wish to use when using hidden commands include:

- *own*
- *purchase*
- *buy*
- *possess*

- *gain*
- *receive*
- *get*

These words used in a hidden command can motivate your prospect to purchase more quickly. For example,

> John, others have decided to *purchase* this program.
>
> Tom, you'll *gain* lot from this.
>
> Jim, others whom I've worked with have *purchased* this plan and have *gotten* great results.

Other salespeople use hidden commands like this:

> A month ago I had a similar question from a friend who was also thinking of *buying this plan.*

In each case, when he said "buying this plan," there was a hidden command in his emphasis.

Hidden commands are used effectively and frequently in newspaper and television advertising. We conjure up immediate emotions when we think of certin products. When Delta Airlines runs its advertisements, it typically advertises not just Delta Airlines but flying Delta. The tag line is "Delta gets you there," not just Delta. The advertisement "Fly Delta" gives you a hidden command.

In Buick commercials, we frequently hear,

> Wouldn't you really rather have a Buick?

The hidden command used in the sentence is "have a Buick."

Hidden commands are all around us. To resist a hidden command would be like resisting breathing.

You, however, can use the same technique to help your prospect buy quickly or at least think about purchasing your product while you communicate.

I know of a securities slesperson who says,

Other investors made a *quick decision*, Steve,

emphasizing the phrase "made a quick decision."

You might think this a very overt technique, but in fact, hidden commands such as these often work very well.

CHAPTER 10

Understanding Your
Prospect's Outcomes

The most important part of any sales communication process is understanding what your prospect really wants. *Outcomes* are not only your prospect's needs and desires but also his perception of what he wants. When your prospect talks to you about buying your product, he's only trying to see, hear, or feel himself with your product in the future. He's trying to imagine the possible outcome of using your product. In this chapter, you'll learn how to discover the outcomes that encompass your prospect's wants and needs.

The Five-Part Outcome-Finding Process

Here is a five-part process for determining your prospect's outcomes and dovetailing them with your own:

1. Let the prospect know what your own outcome is.
2. Ask your prospect for his outcome.
3. Use the "let's assume" fantasy technique.

4. Notice the prospect's nonverbal responses.
5. Work to dovetail both of your outcomes so that you can establish a win-win relationship.

To begin the whole process, you must first establish rapport. Without it, it's pointless to even start to try to get at your prospect's outcomes. It's foolish to think you can even come close to finding out what your prospect wants when trust and credibility have not yet been established.

Letting the Prospect Know Your Own Outcomes

When you have established rapport and trust with your client or prospect, begin by telling him what you want to come of your relationship with him. Present your outcomes to the prospect; tell him what you want from him, what your goals are in being with him. Let him know flatly and outright why you're there to see him. Obviously, telling him that the only reason you are there is to make a $10,000 commission won't do much for your rapport, but if that's the only reason you're there, you won't be much help to him anyway.

Have you ever given *your own* outcome to your prospect? It can really add a personal element to your relationship by showing that you also have needs and desires. When you do it, don't be surprised if the prospect increases his trust in you. Supersalespeople across the country report that when they've satisfied their clients, the clients in turn give them referrals and help them get more business.

In my business of sales training, I often do programs that require me to travel around the country. Sometimes I charge a fairly low fee for my services. I tell my prospects that the reason I am willing to come to present the program at that price is frankly because there are a lot of company executives and meeting planners who will hear me make the presentation. It's a great showcase, and great exposure for me. If I establish rapport and trust and am able to satisfy my prospects' outcomes and they know what my outcomes are, I have found that they are much more likely and prepared to help me accomplish my outcomes.

Asking for Your Prospect's Outcome

After you've established your own outcomes, you should find out what your prospect's desired outcomes are. Many interviews start out with something like this:

As you recall from our phone conversation, Mr.
Prospect, we've discovered ways of lowering your

> taxable income. I've got a few ideas for you that might
> help you achieve these goals.

Unfortunately, the salesperson who uses a line like that has no idea what the prospect's goals really are and definitely has not taken the time to find out what the prospect's outcomes are. When he doesn't know outcomes, he's doomed to failure.

Instead, he should have phrased his opening this way:

> Is lowering taxable income still a top priority for
> you, Ms. Prospect?. . . Why?

Asking your prospect her outcome is perhaps the most important question you could ask. Say something like:

> Now that I've told you what I want, tell me what you
> would like to happen as a result of my services.

Try to phrase the question in a way that helps your prospect use his primary mode of communication, whether it is visual, auditory, or kinesthetic. That will help the person think more quickly.

In simple terms then, the first two steps of the five-part outcome-finding process essentially consist of you saying to your prospects:

> This is what I want. Tell me what you want.

And if you're very sophisticated you'll even try to match the person's visual, auditory, or kinesthetic system:

> This is my goal. Tell me what you'd like to *see* happen
> as a result of our doing business,

or,

> What do you *hear* the results of my services to be?

or,

> What do you *feel* you want as a result of my services?

At this point, there are a couple of things that could happen:

1. Your prospect will tell you exactly what he wants if you are communicating well with him. If you listen attentively, you will arm yourself with the best ammunition you could ever have to wind up winning with a big sale.
2. Your prospect may not know what he wants. In this case, he'll say something like:

How should I know? I haven't thought much about it,

or,

I just don't know what you can do for me. Can you give
   me more information about yourself?

Often, people who don't know what they want are the toughest to sell to because you then have to take additional steps to educate them. Sometimes you must even create or illustrate a need that they probably have not thought of.

In my business as a speaker, I get many referrals to various prospects around the country and around the world. When I call a prospect and tell him what I do and he says that his company is having a conference with 100 people and they would like a speaker on a sales training topic, I know I've done a great job of qualifying and that I've found a prospect who will be very easy to sell to as long as he likes what I have to offer.

On the other hand, if I'm referred to a prospect who has never used a speaker or trainer like me before and hasn't planned a conference in the last couple of years, I know I have my work cut out for me. Very likely I'll have to say something like:

Mr. Prospect, you know that sales congresses can
increase motivation, at least for the short-term in
three or four months. In the long-term, they will
increase sales for your company. This is a very good
investment, Mr. Prospect, because sales will increase
way beyond the amount of money you invest in hotel
rooms, accommodations, and entertainment.

At every step along the way, I've got to try to persuade this prospect of what he might need and want to get an increase in sales. It would be much easier for me to do this by finding a prospect who already knows what he wants and is looking for a way to get it.

People who know and can tell you what they want are the easiest to sell. For example, when my wife and I wanted to buy a new house, we told the realtor the model of house we wanted, which was called a Greenbriar, and the neighborhood we wanted to live in.

Unfortunately, there were no Greenbriars on the market in the community where we wanted to live, so the realtor literally went on foot, knocking at the doors of various Greenbriars and asking their owners if they would like to sell their homes.

Unfortunately, she made one big mistake: She didn't get outcomes from the Greenbriar owners she approached. Instead, she knocked on doors and said,

> I have a buyer who might like to live in this
> neighborhood and likes the floor plan of the
> Greenbriar. Would you be interested in selling your house?

Only two of the forty-three Greenbriar homeowners in the neighborhood were even willing to talk to her. You might think her approach was filled with good old patience and tenacity, but it was probably closer to stupidity.

What if she had approached each of these various owners this way?

> I may have a prospect who is interested in buying your
> Greenbriar. Have you thought of moving to a different
> location, or have you wanted a different style of
> house? What are your plans for the next five years?
> Where would you like to live? Have you thought of an
> investment? Have you thought of other houses in this
> neighborhood? I would like to help you find your next
> house.

Research statistics on relocation suggest that people in the United States move once every five to seven years. If this realtor could have found out the outcomes of the Greenbriar homeowners about new housing, she could have picked up two commissions from the same sale instead of just one from us. Instead, the people who sold us their house bought two condominiums with the proceeds from the sale, with not a penny in commission for our realtor.

Using the "Let's Assume" Fantasy Technique

The third technique in our system for determining outcomes is the *let's-assume fantasy*, a useful tool to help you get your prospect to tell you what he likes best about your product—even if he has never bought a product like yours before.

One of the problems in dealing with a prospect is that it is often difficult to find out how he will buy. The way your prospect bought before is the key to how he will buy in the future, but unfortunately, if he's never bought a product like yours before, you have very little information to go on.

The let's-assume technique allows him to tell you how he will buy in the future.

Another major problem in trying to find a prospect's outcomes is that he often just doesn't know what he wants. A person like this can be a big challenge to a salesperson. But what if you could ask a question that forced him to determine his outcome?

The let's-assume fantasy helps you to sell to this person much faster. You can actually determine his outcome in a matter of minutes.

The let's-assume fantasy is a method for understanding not only your prospect's needs but his dreams, and it allows you to find out how to turn those dreams into realistic and attainable goals. A let's-assume fantasy puts your prospect into the future with your product by forcing him to think one hour, one month, or ten years ahead—to imagine what he liked about the product or how it helped him. When you find out these answers, they'll point you in the right direction for your sales approach.

For example, you say to your prospect,

> Let's just assume that our discussion about Product X
> has ended. What has happened during this interview to
> let you know that the time was well spent?

The prospect might respond:

> You listened to what my needs are for products and you
> also gave me some good information to use in making a
> decision about how Product X will solve my problem. You
> also let me know the pricing structures and the financing
> available on Product X. If I assume right now that our
> discussion is over, these are the things that I've
> learned.

Or, in a real estate sales situation, you might say,

> Let's assume that it's six months down the road. What
> has occurred during that six-month period to let you know
> that this house was a good buy for you?

You may get responses such as these:

Well, the house we bought appreciated $20,000 in six months.

My family likes it.

Nothing fell apart.

You'll notice that each of these responses reflects different needs and wants. One person is interested in the house as an investment, another is concerned about the comfort of the family, while still another cares primarily about the upkeep of the house and how well it's put together.

With a tax shelter product, you might ask,

Assume that you've had this investment for one year. What has happened that first year to let you know it was right for you?

Your prospect might respond,

One year has elapsed and the tax shelter appreciated 18 percent, just as you said it would.

Nothing happened to make me lose money on this deal. That's what I like about it.

As you can see, the prospect will literally hand you the outcome he hopes for. If you can get your prospect to do some future planning and let you know exactly what he wants from your product or service, all you have to do is find a way to give it back to him. It's almost like someone handing you money without you doing any work for it. When you discover what the prospect's fantasies are, you can then present the product benefits that best appeal to him.

This can make even salespeople with very little talent incredibly successful. It is the most valuable probing technique you can use, because it is guaranteed to give you your prospect's real objectives or hot buttons to hit to get them to respond. The let's-assume technique literally allows you to see how your prospect decided to buy your product even though he hasn't bought it yet.

If you want to add a touch of sophistication to the let's-assume technique, you might try matching your prospect's thought mode when getting his outcomes. For instance, to a kinesthetic you could say,

Let's assume that it is six months into the future.
What has happened to make you *feel* you got a good
deal?

To a visual you'd say,

> Let's assume you've owned this for six months. In your
> *view*, what did you like the best about it?

Or, to an auditory,

> Let's say it's six months into the future. What has
> happened to make this *sound* like a good deal to you now?

I used this technique with a sales manager at Blue Cross. He was procrastinating about whether to use me for a summer program. I quickly realized that I didn't quite know what his outcomes were. I decided to ask him one question:

> Bill, what do you really see yourself wanting for your
> salespeople? What do you envision will do them the most
> good?

He responded,

> Well, gee, I'd like to see them be more motivated and
> make more sales calls. I'd like to see them to work
> more effectively, "work smarter, not harder," and
> generally improve their self-esteem.

Well, I realized right there that Bill's analysis of what his people needed was like a wish list stretching from the earth to the moon. His response was just as useless to me as if he'd said he didn't know. He had really given me too much information to be of any help.

I decided to help him do some future planning or as-if fantasizing. I said,

> Bill, lets pretend we've completed the program and
> it's six months afterward. What about the presentation
> program makes it look as if it worked for you?

Bill got very specific. He said,

> Well, the salespeople have a higher activity level. I
> see that they've increased their sales by 25 percent,
> and it appears that they have more company loyalty.

From those choice pieces of information, I was able to tailor my comments exactly to what Bill wanted to hear: I gave him testimonials from other companies in the same industry that had experienced sales increases of more than 25 percent after my presentations. In many cases, the increases were as high as 70, 80, and 90 percent. I showed him letters from salespeople who had increased their activity by 200 to 300 percent for a period directly after my presentation. In fact, I even found one letter specifically saying that the salespeople had increased their loyalty and gratitude toward the sales manager for bringing in such a fine speaker.

I got the booking, but if I hadn't used the let's-assume technique, I can guarantee that it wouldn't have been as easy.

Noticing Your Prospect's Nonverbal Responses

The fourth way to understand your prospect's outcomes and find out what he is thinking while you're asking questions or probing is to notice the nonverbal cues and responses he gives you.

I've discussed nonverbal cues such as crossing legs, crossing arms, leaning forward, and leaning backward, but there are much more specific and sophisticated nonverbal cues.

There are literally hundreds of muscles in the face that will change depending on the expression the individual wants to use. No one expression means the same for everybody, but each expression has a unique meaning to the person who makes it.

For example, a raised eyebrow may mean one kind of surprise to one person and a different kind of surprise to another. The same may be true of skin color and tone.

In almost every prospect, not only do pupils dilate during periods of enthusiasm and excitement but skin color lightens during periods of high enthusiasm.

You must *calibrate* to find out what your prospect looks like when he's happy or how he appears when he is sad. If you can do this, you will be much more effective in knowing what your prospect is thinking when you talk with him.

In my seminars, I frequently conduct exercises with a dollar bill. I ask one individual to open her hands as wide as possible while the other individual holds the dollar bill and tries to get it in between her partner's index finger and thumb. The trick is that both partners must look at each other's eyes and not at the dollar bill. This forces the viewer to notice minute skin-color and muscle-tone changes in the face. Most people have an extremely difficult time doing this, but after five or ten minutes of practice, almost everyone catches the dollar bill in her fingers at least 50 percent of the time.

By paying very close attention to your partner's unique skin-color and muscle-tone changes, you will find it is almost like reading your prospect's mind.

Dovetailing Your Outcome With That of Your Prospect

The fifth step in using outcomes is to dovetail your outcome with the outcome of your prospect. There is a negotiation paradigm that always works, and that's the concept of the "win-win."

In the old sales model, the prospect and the salesperson are in competition, where one person is destined to win and the other to lose. Some people believe that in any deal, "win-lose" always has been and always will be the case. But really the opposite is true.

If you let your prospect know what you want and what will make you win, he'll help you win as long as you do the same for him. This is what is meant by *dovetailing outcomes.* There's nothing wrong with having your prospect know that you want a commission for a job well done if at the same time you assure him that you'll do your level best to help him to get what he wants.

Let me give you an example of how this five-step outcome formula works. I spoke to a group called The National Association of Health Underwriters, a health organization dedicated to helping its members get more education and attain higher levels of professionalism. It also serves as a forum for networking and political activities. Rod was the program chairman referred to me. Here is the discussion Rod and I had:

ME: Rod, as we discussed, Tim referred me to you, thinking that you might be able to use a sales consultant on your next convention program.

ROD: Well, I respect Tim's advice and suggestions.

ME: Rod, I want to speak at this convention, obviously because I make a fee, but also because it's the type of program that will generate referrals and company business for me. What I really want to know is, what kind of speaker do you think would best fit into your plans?

ROD: I don't know. I guess a speaker who is well-known would draw people in. I can't *see* having a speaker in an empty room.

ME: Well Rod, that makes sense, but to give me more information on what you want, let's assume that the convention is over. What did you *see* happen that let you know the speaker was successful?

ROD: Well, let's *see.* I *see* the attendees walking up to me saying it was the best convention they ever attended. The speaker was entertaining but informative, and he involved the audience so well that the attendees felt like part of the program.

ME: Ah, so your *view* is that you want a speaker who is entertaining and informative and involves the audience in the program. Is that the way you *see* it?

ROD: Yes. That's exactly it.

ME: Good. Let me show you some recommendation letters from groups who said that they found each of those three things in my programs.

I did speak at that program. Rod helped me to get my outcome and appreciated my letting him know what that outcome was. But more important, even though he didn't know what he wanted, I got Rod to do some future planning with me. I found out exactly what his needs and wants were and helped him to that same discovery as well. The end result was that I got a generous fee and a lot of referrals; it was the perfect program for both of us. And that's what I mean by win-win or dovetailing outcomes.

Did you notice that during my conversation with Rod I used the visual, instead of the auditory or kinesthetic, mode as part of the future planning? I tried to match Rod's thinking mode. Did you detect what mode Rod was using? He said,

Let me *see*. I *see* the attendees walking up to me.

Of course, he was a visual. So as I talked to him, I tried to help him visualize. I said,

So your *view* is that you want a speaker who is informative and entertaining. Is that the way you *see* it? Let me *show* you some recommendation letters for you to *look at*.

Use these strategies. They will really work for you.

I talked to a financial products salesperson who used the let's-assume technique on three different business executives whom he was trying to get to invest some money. He said that this one single technique—the let's-assume future planning technique—netted him $50,000 in commissions in half the time it would usually take to do that kind of business.

Why? Because he told each prospect his outcome. He said he wanted to do a good job because he wanted to get referrals. He then found out what his prospect's outcome was. He used the let's-assume fantasy to determine both wants and needs. He watched his prospect's thinking mode, and he dovetailed outcomes to support a win-win situation.

There is nothing new about the win-win concept. But by understanding how the concept works psychologically, you are better-prepared to reach that goal and gain rapport with your prospect. Opportunities will flow to you in rapid order if you know what your prospect's outcomes are. On the other hand, your sales efforts will absolutely fail without this information.

It has long been said that if you can help people get what they want, they will help you get what you want. This chapter focuses on that same altruistic, yet profitable, idea.

The Benefits of Discovering Outcomes

Here are some benefits you'll gain from discovering your prospect's outcomes:

- You'll find out how to let your prospect help you get what you really want.
- You'll find out how to elicit your prospect's outcomes in his own thought mode: visual, auditory, or kinesthetic. In other words, you'll get him to let you know what he wants in his most natural way of thinking.
- You'll find ways to speed up the sales process or get a deal settled more quickly by establishing agreement.

Using the concept of outcomes is powerful but so easy that you may think it seems too easy. It takes the challenge out of persuasion.

Eliciting outcomes is diametrically opposed to the manipulative sales strategies used by salespeople of old, complete with white buck shoes and white belt, reminiscent of Willy Loman in Arthur Miller's *Death of a Salesman*. This type of salesperson will try to talk you into doing what *he* wants you to do. Today's more sophisticated salespeople realize that you have to *listen* the prospect into doing what you'd like him to do as opposed to *telling* him what you'd like him to do. The process of listening is vital to your sales efforts, but it is not enough to ferret out the unique information: that specific communication by which your prospect lets you know exactly what he or she wants.

Outcomes vs. Needs

Understanding your prospect's outcomes is incredibly powerful and highly underused, but be careful not to confuse outcomes with needs. Getting outcomes is more powerful than just understanding needs, because once you find them out, you'll understand not only his needs but his fantasies. You'll understand his goals and desires as well.

A need is what the prospect *thinks* he wants at the time. An outcome includes what the prospect wanted in the past, what he wants in the present, *and* what he may want in the future. If you identify a prospect's outcomes, it will not only tell you what the prospect wants and how you should sell it to him but also, if you are really uncovering outcomes, how he bought before and how he will buy right now. You will even be able to determine how he will buy in the future.

You should also realize, however, that probing and finding outcomes is the most important part of the sales process. This is even more important than cashing objections (see Chapter 13) and closing (see Chapter 16). If you adequately learn your prospect's outcomes—that is, what he wants and what he will buy—you'll never have to use objection-handling techniques. You will only need to know when to stop the interview and write out the order.

When you've established enough trust and loyalty with your customers to show them that you know what they really want, then they will trust you to sell them what you, through your professional expertise, think they really need.

By discussing outcomes, you will find out both what they want *and* what they need at once. And if you strive to help prospects get what they want, they in turn will help you get exactly what you want.

CHAPTER 11

The Instant Replay Technique

Using the *instant replay technique*, you will be able to discover your prospects' buying strategies and know exactly what processes they use in making decisions about your product. Those buying strategies and decision-making processes are deeply influenced by how they have made decisions about products they've purchased in the past. Once you understand that people's future decisions are similar to their past decisions, you will be able to increase your sales significantly.

Do People Change?

One of the fundamental beliefs coming from modern psychology is that people typically change their basic personality and behavior patterns very little through the years. Much of the current knowledge available in the field of developmental psychology comes from psychological researcher Jean Piaget. Piaget determined that basic personality patterns are developed between ages 2 and 7. How you behave between those ages is a significant predictor of how you will react and behave throughout the rest of your life.

Obviously, maturity sets in and changes some behavioral responses, but most psychological research is built upon the simple idea that it is extremely difficult to change.

If you were able to change quickly, it would cause so much stress that you would develop ulcers, palpitations, headaches, and a myriad of other psychological problems.

Psychologists can actually predict what will happen to you if you change too much. You can have something as bad as a heart attack or a symptom as minor as headaches just by the amount of change you have had in your life.

The Life Events and Social Readjustment Rating Scale

To give you an idea just how stressful change in our lives can be, psychiatric researcher, Thomas Holmes, has developed a test to show you how much stress you will have depending on the changes in your life within a two-year period. He calls it the Life Events and Social Readjustment Rating Scale, shown in Exhibit 4. Note the number of behavior changes that can cause stress in a person's life.

Take a few minutes to see how you score on Holmes' scale. Remember, the scale registers both negative stress (e.g., job firings, divorces, death in the family) and positive stress (e.g., vacations, weddings, births). When stress is compounded, whether it is positive or negative, it contributes to your overall stress level.

How did you score?

- If you scored *between 0 and 100*, it indicates that there is a low level of change in your life.
- If you scored between *100 and 200*, there is a possibility that a major illness could occur to you within the next two years.
- If you scored *between 200 and 500*, a major illness could occur within the next year.
- If you scored *500 or over*, you have a high propensity toward physical and psychological disease or illness.

We don't like change. Think about it. Hasn't your behavior pattern generally been the same in the past as it is today?

By using the instant replay technique, you avoid causing your prospects stress. The technique of selling prospects the way they want to be sold is not new, but understanding what causes them to act as they do can help us gain a deeper understanding and a higher level of trust and rapport with prospects.

EXHIBIT 4. *Holmes' Life Events and Social Readjustment Rating Scale.*

Change puts distinct strain on stress-coping mechanisms. When such events accumulate, the chances for stress-linked disorders tend to increase. The Life Change Unit (LCU) values below suggest relative impact of various common life change events.

WORK

Being fired from work	____ × 47 =	____
Retirement from work	____ × 45 =	____
Major business adjustment	____ × 39 =	____
Changing to different line of work	____ × 36 =	____
Major change in work responsibilities	____ × 29 =	____
*Trouble with boss	_1_ × 23 =	____
Major change in working conditions	____ × 20 =	____

PERSONAL

Major personal injury or illness	____ × 53 =	____
Outstanding personal achievement	____ × 23 =	____
*Major revision of personal habits	_1_ × 24 =	____
*Major change in recreation	_1_ × 19 =	____
*Major change in church activities	_1_ × 19 =	____
*Major change in sleeping habits	_1_ × 16 =	____
*Major change in eating habits	_1_ × 15 =	____
Vacation	____ × 13 =	____

FINANCIAL

*Major change in financial state	_1_ × 38 =	____
Mortgage or loan over $50,000	____ × 31 =	____
Mortgage foreclosure	____ × 30 =	____
Mortgage or loan under $50,000	____ × 17 =	____

FAMILY

Death of a spouse	____ ×100 =	____
Divorce	____ × 73 =	____
Marital separation	____ × 65 =	____
Death of a close relative	____ × 63 =	____
Marriage	____ × 50 =	____
Marital reconciliation	____ × 45 =	____

Major change in health of family	_____ × 44 =	_____
Pregnancy	_____ × 40 =	_____
Addition of new family member	_____ × 39 =	_____
*Major change in arguments with spouse	__1__ × 35 =	_____
Son or daughter leaving home	_____ × 29 =	_____
*In-law problems	__1__ × 29 =	_____
Spouse starting or ending work	_____ × 26 =	_____
*Major change in family get-togethers	__1__ × 15 =	_____

SOCIAL

Detention in jail	_____ × 63 =	_____
*Sexual difficulties	__1__ × 39 =	_____
Death of a close friend	_____ × 37 =	_____
Start or end of formal schooling	_____ × 26 =	_____
Major change in living conditions	_____ × 25 =	_____
Changing to a new school	_____ × 20 =	_____
Change in residence	_____ × 20 =	_____
*Change in social activities	__1__ × 18 =	_____
Minor violations of the law	_____ × 11 =	_____

*If the event has an asterisk next to it, has it happened to you at least once within the last two years? If the answer is yes, multiply the value by 1 and enter the total in the space provided. If "no", leave it blank.

If the event has no asterisk next to it, and it has happened to you during the past two years, multiply the value by the number of times it has occurred—for example, "Being fired from work" twice would be entered as 2 × 47 = 94.

How to Use the Instant Replay Technique

To use the instant replay technique, all you need to do is ask your prospect a very simple question:

How did you decide to buy Product X in the past?

or,

What made you decide to buy this product in the past?

This is precisely the technique that an insurance agent I know used on his prospect. This is how his prospect responded:

> I bought that policy in the past because the company
> was one that I recognized. They promised cash value
> that would be pegged to the prime rate, and the agent
> promised me he would follow up at least once a year and
> stay interested in me.

With those three reasons, the insurance agent had it made. He waited until he got through the probing interview. But take a guess at what high points he focused on when he presented his product?

It was simple. All he said was:

> Well, this company has been around for about sixty years.
> It's a company you should recognize. It pays cash
> values pegged to the same rate as the prime rate, and I
> promise that I will keep in contact with you at least
> once a year.

Another useful follow-up question to ask a prospect is:

> If you did it all over again, how would you improve
> this product?

Then you get not only past behavior patterns but also a product wish list.

By using the instant replay technique, all you are really doing is getting a buying strategy from that person. You assume that he will buy in the future in a fashion similar to the way he bought in the past. You've taken the information he gives you and have played it back to him. Denying you would be like denying himself.

Let me give you an example of how I've used this technique. A company president in the financial services industry whose name is Charlie once talked to me about doing training for his brokers. In the past he had used a psychologist from Laguna Beach, California, who had spoken on self-image. I used the instant replay technique on Charlie:

ME: How did you decide to go with this guy before? What made you decide to go with him?

CHARLIE: Well, Mike was referred to me by one of our brokers. Our brokers liked his humorous speaking style and his presentation content. But he was

also willing to prorate travel expenses to our various offices. He was motivating because he told a lot of stories to illustrate his ideas.

ME: What is one thing you would like to improve in the presentation from this
guy?

CHARLIE: Well, I guess the only thing I'd like to improve is to get Mike to
tailor his message a little bit more to the specific needs of our group.

All of this information was useful to me in giving Charlie exactly what he
wanted. I replayed the information I'd obtained during the probing or interview-
ing period and showed him recommendations and testimonial letters from people
who thought I was good at motivating, using humorous stories, and, more important, tailoring my message to a group's individual needs. I assured him that
I would prorate expenses. All I needed to do was to convince Charlie that that
was exactly what he wanted. I did, and I got the business.

The instant replay technique uses probing as a tool, but it goes a step further.
By finding your prospect's past strategy, in addition to answering his needs, you
can also allow him to buy the way he's bought before. You're not only filling
his needs but making the buying situation less stressful. If you can find out your
buyer's strategy and replay it to him, he'll give you the business you want.

But be careful. The instant replay technique can be very manipulative if used
in the wrong way. You can't just play back a prospect's buying strategy with
empty promises. You must in reality be able to deliver the goods. And you don't
want to play back false information just to suit your own needs either. If you
did, you'd be selling a product that the prospect doesn't need or want. In the
long run, not being honest is a lousy strategy.

Use the instant replay technique carefully and honestly and your closing rate
will rise rapidly.

CHAPTER 12

How to Use
Psychological Sliding

Psychological sliding is a solid sales technique that can help you when you are having difficulty selling.

Has a prospect ever frozen on an objection or an attitude and then become so rigid that you couldn't move him off of his objection? Here's where psychological sliding comes into play.

Psychological sliding is a technique for moving your prospect from one thought pattern to another. It helps him sell himself so that you can psychologically move him away from his objections instead of fighting him point by point.

As a communication device, psychological sliding appears elegant and effortless. It is a way to help your prospect experience the product you are selling in more than one thought mode.

Sliding Your Prospect Away
From Objections

Even though your prospect may be a visual and like to think in individual pictures and use visual words, he also can freeze on an objection in the visual mode as well. When he has an objection, it is usually as a picture of something going wrong or a photograph of why your product won't work.

If you want to slide a visual prospect away from an objection, the best technique is to change that objectionable picture into a feeling or a sound. Slide your prospect into his nonprimary mode, where there's a chance that he may not have the same objection. Even though your prospect may be fundamentally visual-based, he can still think in an auditory or kinesthetic mode if he has to. By sliding the prospect away from the objection he has in one mode of communication, you might be able to sell him in another mode.

Take the example of someone trying to sell an expensive car. Here's an experience I had at a BMW dealership. As I was shopping for a new car, a salesman walked up to me:

SALESMAN: Nice car, huh?
ME: Yeah, real nice.
S: What do you like best about it?
ME: Well, I guess it's the way it performs, its power and handling.
S: Would you like to sit in it?
ME: Yeah, I've driven it before, but I'd love to try again.
S: Do you feel you'd like to own it?
ME: Well, I think it has a little too much power for my needs. The 325 would probably suit me just as well. And frankly, the 325 is just a little less expensive.
S: This really is a nicer car than the 325. I think you'd feel that you should have bought this in the end.
ME: No, no. I think I'll go compare prices on the 325 and give you a call in a few days, okay?
S: That's fine, but just out of curiosity, do you feel that your image is important to you?
ME: Well, sure.
S: Can you see the difference between a 325 and a 535i on the road?
ME: Well, you bet.
S: A professional in public view like you needs to keep up a good image, right?
ME: Yeah.

S: Well, I would venture to guess that when you drive to a presentation or meeting, the attendees get an idea of the level of your success by the way you look, right?

ME: Well, okay. But what are you getting at?

S: Well, since you can see the differences in the two models, other people, possibly your prospective clients, will see those differences as well. Let me ask you something. If you could get one or two more clients because of the enhanced image you'll get from owning this car, then do you feel you'd like to own this car?

ME: Hmm. . . . Well. You bet. Sold!

In this example, the salesman could tell that I was kinesthetic from the responses I gave when he asked what I liked about the car. My response was "power and handling," which pertain to how the car feels. He found me objecting to the car because I didn't need that much power, so he slid me into the visual aspects of the car and found my hot buttons by asking me what else I liked.

He realized the objection was kinesthetic. I said it had too much power. Instead of saying it really didn't have that much power, he moved me into a visual mode:

> You care about your image, don't you?

> Can you see the difference between a 325 and a 535i on the road?

and he tried to close me kinesthetically by saying,

> Do you feel you'd like to own this car?

I had objected that the car cost too much, and he tried to counter the objection. But I almost left, saying I was going to compare prices, so he switched channels or thinking modes: He used a psychological slide to the visual mode by asking me how I felt about my image—combining feeling with image. Of course, I care about my image! So he successfully slid me away from my kinesthetic objections so that I would see visual benefits. The psychological sliding technique works with any product. The BMW salesman realized I was blocking or objecting in my kinesthetic mode, so he slid me into my visual mode where I didn't have the same objections. After all, I had no objections to its looks, only to the excess power.

Steps to Effective Psychological Sliding

There are three basic steps to using psychological sliding effectively.

1. *Begin by addressing your client or prospect and commenting on his focus of attention.* Start by saying something like (in our car example):

> Isn't this a nice car?

instead of the usual,

> Can I help you?

Or,

> Can I help you look for something, today?

Don't be too abrupt, or the customer may give a standard response:

> No thanks, just looking.

Slide, don't jump.

2. *When you sense that your prospect is blocking with an objection, slide smoothly to another sensory mode.* For example, go from feeling to seeing, kinesthetic to visual. The same objection may not exist in another thought mode. If the prospect says,

> It *looks* like it's too much for me,

you can counter by saying,

> Do you *feel* you'd like to own it?

3. *Try to help the client experience the new thought mode as much as possible.* Using our car example, you might get the prospect to experience the visuals of the car by talking about how nice the car would look in her driveway or how the prospect would look driving down the street in such a gorgeous car. All of these visual images should conjure up desires to own it and counter the objections.

Psychological sliding works for any sales professional. A fairly seasoned broker was trying to explain the structure of a financial product to her client. The broker determined that her client's primary mode of communication was visual, so she drew pictures, charts, and produced illustrations that were provided by her company.

She could tell, however, that the client's interest was waning by the time she came to the end of her presentation. So she asked him if he had any concerns. True to his visual form, he said,

I don't see it fitting my goals.

"Why do you say that?" the broker asked.

Well, I saw some bad publicity on the company.

The broker put away her illustrations, charts, and graphs, and psychologically slid him into the kinesthetic mode.

Ed, I've had clients about your age making about
the same income as you who still feel grateful that
they invested with the company.

She moved closer, touched him on the arm, and shared her feelings about the company's management leadership.

By her being able to slide his focus of attention from a visual to a kinesthetic mode, Ed became more thoughtful and contemplative and less preoccupied with his initial objection. Finally, he said,

Well, if you have that much faith in this company,
I'll trust it too.

Granted, psychological sliding will not always work. There are times when even sliding a prospect from one mode of communication to another will not result in a sale and you will have to make use of some of the other subliminal selling techniques to build rapport with the prospect. Sometimes, a prospect simply may not be ready to buy. But psychological sliding is especially helpful when you are trying to sell to rigid or inflexible people. Individuals who don't understand the benefits right away will respond very nicely to psychological sliding. The technique is also effective with indecisive people or people who need to be led a little bit more.

Psychological sliding is one of the most sophisticated yet simple principles in sales psychology. The next time you face a difficult objection from a prospect, try psychological sliding. It will give you a useful tool to help you increase your closing rate.

CHAPTER 13

Cashing In: Turning
Objections Into Sales

Has a prospect ever made an objection you couldn't counter? Or given you an objection that seemed foolish to you? There are subliminal selling skills you can use to *cash* objections and turn them into sales.

Take, for example, the following conversation between a health insurance salesman and his client:

SALESMAN: Before I leave, I'd like to get a quick medical history on you.
CLIENT: Wait a second. I'm really having a problem with the premium price. It's really too much.
S: Yes, but it's a great policy. In the end, you'd be sorry that you didn't act quickly.
CLIENT: I don't think that I can afford the premium. It's just too much.
S: Now, it's really not that much. It's only $5 a day. You can handle that, can't you?
CLIENT: No. Let me think about it and get back to you.

Do you think the prospect eventually gave the salesman the business? If you don't, you're absolutely right.

What did the salesman do wrong? Could he have cashed this objection instead of wasting his and his prospect's time?

What really were the prospect's objections? Objections are very valuable in letting you know what your prospect is thinking. They also provide valuable information about whether you are satisfying your prospect's needs.

A lot of salespeople are much too talkative. They don't listen enough, so they never really know their prospect's needs or desires and spend all their time telling him what they've got and how important it is to him, even though they don't know what he needed in the first place.

Three Steps to Cashing Objections

Here are three steps to cashing objections, three steps that will give you the opportunity to literally turn an objection into money:

1. Acknowledge the objection.
2. Uncover the intent behind the objection.
3. Resolve it subliminally.

Acknowledging the Objection

First, acknowledge the objection. You've got to listen carefully to your prospect's voice: how low, how soft, or how hard is it?

Next, pace the objection. Your prospect has a frame of reference in which he gives you the objection. Use that to begin your answer.

For example, I was cold-called at my office by Ed, a computer salesman. He walked into the office and as he was talking to the secretary, I left my inner office to see what was going on. I told Ed that I had enough computers but that the property and casualty insurance agent across the hall from me had a deep need. I escorted Ed to the insurance office. After the introduction, George, the insurance agent, listened to Ed for about ten seconds and said,

Computers are really too expensive for me right now,

to which Ed responded,

It costs you not to have one.

Ed had missed the whole point. He hadn't seen past the objection and had mismatched. Instead, if he had said,

> You're right. They are expensive. But would you agree
> that in the end it may be expensive not to have one?

he would have acknowledged much more elegantly that he cared about George's initial objection.

If you don't acknowledge the objection, you'll only get into a tug-of-war of egos that you, the salesperson, can never win.

You should also double-check your rapport. How are you sitting? Where are you sitting? Are you within 2 feet of your prospect? Where are his hands? Eyes? Arms? Are you matching and mirroring while he is giving you his objections?

Uncovering the Meaning and Intent Behind the Objection

The second step is to uncover the meaning and intent behind the objection. You've got to understand what the prospect is *really* thinking behind what he says.

In other words, listen between the lines.

Often, the objection is just a ruse to cover a fear of giving you the go-ahead. The prospect may think that it's appropriate to object to show that she doesn't give in too quickly, but in most cases, it's just a fear of change, a fear of making a decision.

From now on, uncover the real meaning of a prospect's objection. Find the intent behind the objection this way:

> That's an interesting comment. Why did you bring that
> up?

Asking this one question will ferret out the real meaning behind almost every objection.

When I first entered the consulting business, I went to an insurance agency in Los Angeles. The general agent, Bruce, quickly made an objection after just a few moments of my presentation:

BRUCE: We just had a speaker recently. I can't use you.

ME: I see. Why is that a factor?

BRUCE: Well, we just used this guy. He was well-liked, but we didn't get an increase in sales. It was just entertainment with no benefit.

I proceeded to prove to him how insurance agencies I had worked with had increased their sales.

BRUCE: Your approach is very interesting. Let's talk more about it.

If I had not ferreted out his real meaning and intent by asking,

> Why is this important to you?

or,

> Why do you bring that up?

I would have been walking out the door before I had had a chance to walk in.

Testing the Importance of the Objection and Resolving It Subliminally

The third step in answering or cashing objections is to test the importance of the objection and resolve it subliminally.

Remember to match your prospect's thought mode visually, auditorially, or kinesthetically whenever you have to cash an objection.

Unless you like to get into verbal boxing matches with your prospects, you've probably realized that you are not paid to explain, you are paid to close. You need to find out very quickly if your prospect is committed to solving his own needs.

Start by asking,

> Is that all that's standing in your way in going
> along with this?

or,

> If we get past this point can we write this up?

or,

> If I can answer this to your satisfaction, can I go
> ahead with this?

If your prospect says "No" or "I don't know," it's probably just a ruse. He is likely feeling other roadblocks or dissatisfactions behind the objections he's made to you. He's not committed. Go back and find out his real needs, since you probably haven't done an adequate job of probing him. Go back and reestablish his goals and outcomes.

I once heard of a salesman who was with a prospect for almost three straight hours. For ninety minutes of those three hours, he answered objection after objection. He could have short-circuited the whole process after the first objection by asking,

> Is this the only thing that's bothering you?

or,

> If we get past this, could we write this up?

If you can't get a commitment like that, go back and problem-solve again. Look for more information to find out what the prospect really wants, not what you think he wants.

Rephrasing Objections

Another way to cash objections is to rephrase them. It's possible that an objection can be turned into a benefit if you reword or rephrase it correctly.

The objection could even become very useful as the basis for satisfying another need. For example, the Cadillac salesman might ask,

> What do you think of this beautiful car?

The objection might be,

> It's too heavy.

The Cadillac salesman would then say,

Well, it may be heavy, but it has road-hugging
weight.

An insurance buyer's objection might be,

The premiums are too high.

The insurance salesman can then reframe the objection and say,

Well, you're right. But high premiums usually mean
quality protection from a well-established, financially
solid company.

One of my favorite objections in my business come from those prospects
who say,

We don't use speakers.

I counter by asking,

Do you use consultants?

In other words, I reframe my position to correspond to something that they can
more closely identify with.

Diffusion

Another technique is something called *diffusion* or *disassociation*. All of us, from
time to time, get negative reactions from prospects when we try to close. They
might even make an objection that is more than a little irritating.

I remember talking to the vice-president of training for a major airline in
San Diego. After about forty-five minutes into the conversation, it was obvious
to me that I had what he needed:

ME: Well, why don't you give me a 25 percent retainer right now and we'll
start today?

He responded by giving me an extremely negative objection:

VP: We haven't even covered my real needs yet. Now, how can you think that you know exactly what our needs are?

Obviously, I had chosen the wrong time to close. I then disassociated myself from my mistake:

ME: You're right. I do need to get a lot more information. Tell me more about your staff's biggest weaknesses.

I had quickly disassociated myself from the objection by saying,

> You're right, let's get more information.

I then paced him by asking a question about his staff. His mind was still on his training problems. I had simply tried to close too quickly, but I got myself out and closed later more successfully.

Answering
the Prospect's Needs

When cashing objections, remember that your goal is to select a solution that answers the prospect's true needs and stays within the context of his questions. If you solve his needs and he knows you're solving them, you'll get many fewer objections than you might expect.

Early in this chapter I tell about the encounter between a health insurance agent and his client. Do you remember the mistakes the salesman made? How could the salesman have used the cashing techniques you've learned in this chapter?

Let's rejoin the salesman as he deals with his prospect by cashing the objections instead of letting them sit on the table unanswered:

S: Ah, before I leave, I'd like to get a quick medical history on you.
CLIENT: Wait a second! I'm really having a problem with the premium price. It's really too much.

[*At this point, the salesman checks on his rapport with the prospect, including body position and voice quality.*]

S: I hear you saying the price is a little high. Is this a big concern for you?

[*He is resolving the objection subliminally by centering on the prospect's auditory mode.*]

CLIENT: Well, sure. I don't want to pay more than I have to. It's not crucial. But my father-in-law is an ex-insurance agent. He told me that the premiums are about $1 per $1,000 of coverage for permanent insurance. Your policy is about five times that expensive.

[*The prospect is getting a little bit suspicious because the father-in-law probably bragged about cheap insurance. The insurance salesman suddenly remembers that his prospect's outcome is to get basic protection for his family.*]

S: I understand that cost is important to you. Do you remember that you indicated protection as an important factor in purchasing this policy? Does that still *ring* true?
CLIENT: Well, yes, but I still don't want to pay too much.
S: I understand your concern about paying too much for insurance. And to reach my recommendation on which product would best suit your needs, I took into consideration not only price but your desire to give your family the best possible protection available. However, I was worried about one thing.
CLIENT: What's that?
S: Well, I could have used cheaper products from other companies, but a couple or years ago I did that for a family like yours. . . . and the insurer eventually went out of business. It was very tough for the client to get insurance and straighten out the premiums and policies, even though I was there every step of the way. In the end, we went to an established company with a great reputation—and, of course, more reasonable premiums in the end. How does that sound to you?
CLIENT: I guess my father-in-law is a little bit behind the times.
S: Should we get back to the medical history?
CLIENT: You bet.

Following steps like these to cash objections, you'll get a lot more business because you will be telling the prospect what he wants to hear, the way he wants to hear it. And you won't ever have to knock your head against the wall in the process.

The salesman in the example used metaphors and stories to help cash objections. To illustrate his point, he told the story of another couple who went with a cheaper insurance product. Metaphors and stories are powerful tools. In Chapter 14, you'll learn how they can be used to effectively close sales.

Objection-Cashing Pointers

Here are a few questions to ask yourself when cashing an objection:

- Have I established rapport?
- Am I voice matching?
- Am I using other subliminal selling skills I've read about in this book?
- Do I know the prospect's outcome for the meeting?
- Do I know what he really wants from me?
- Have I listened well enough to gain information about the prospect's needs?
- Have I matched my product's benefits to fit the prospect's needs?
- Have I given the prospect exactly the benefits he needs to understand why my product is important to him?

CHAPTER 14

Stories
and Metaphors

Metaphors and stories help your prospect to see, hear, and feel himself in the pictures you create. A *metaphor* is a figure of speech or a verbal association that may help the listener to better understand the concept you are trying to explain. An example of a metaphor is the expression: "The salesman is a rock." Well, obviously, the salesman is not a piece of stone, but the listener forms an impression of a well-established person with a solid reputation—generally a steady character. Metaphors allow the listener to grasp immediately what the speaker is trying to say.

A story works similarly, but perhaps not as quickly. By using a story about how others who have used a product or service have achieved their sought-after goals, you reassure the prospect so he can envision himself in the subject of the story's place. Any verbal association or story that leads him to identify or see himself in your ideas helps that prospect understand your ideas much faster.

How Metaphors Work to Make You Money

Metaphors and stories work to make you money in the sales process in four basic ways:

1. *By deeply gripping your listener's attention.* He is listening emotionally to an interesting story or a fascinating concept, not just to dry facts.
2. *By simplifying ideas so that they are sharper through comparison and example.* Even the brightest person loves simple, easy-to-understand concepts, because they enable him to understand complex concepts through the new understanding you've given him.
3. *By getting your listener's emotions going.* If you can use the right metaphor to get the prospect to see himself in the situation where he has a positive experience using your product, he'll go for it.
4. *By being memorable.* Your prospect may forget the facts, but he'll remember your stories and illustrations.

A very bright, sharp financial planner told my wife and me an incredibly effective story when we were evaluating an investment:

> Kerry, I have a client who really fits into the same
> tax bracket as you and Sandy. This client was making
> about as much as you were ten years ago before he bought into
> these mutual funds we're talking about today.
> I have to tell you now that he has enough income
> coming in to support two houses as well as enough money
> to have purchased a sailboat last year. To tell you the
> truth, he and his wife are sailing their 40-fort ketch
> around the Hawaiian Islands at this very moment.
> They decided to take two years off and just sail
> around the world.

This story was especially effective with me since I loved to sail, and the financial planner knew it. He also knew through previous conversations that one of my fantasies was sailing a boat for a long distance. He happened to use the story about his clients taking an extended vacation in their 40-foot ketch at directly the right place in his presentation by making it appear that the mutual fund investment made their dreams come true.

The timing of the story was masterful, and the financial planner made a sale. Knowing that I wanted to pay for sailing with my investment income forced me to say yes to practically anything he had to offer that day.

In the speaking profession, most speakers use a lot of metaphors and stories to get the audience to identify more quickly with the point the speaker is trying to make. People love stories.

A life insurance agent in Detroit has an uncanny way of using metaphors in the right way when he sells whole-life insurance. He once told a carpet retailer,

> To tell you the truth, the difference between whole
> life and term is like the difference between indoor and
> outdoor carpeting. Both look nice, but one lasts a whole
> lot longer and gives you more benefits in the end.

If you can tailor your message to your prospect's jargon, reference points, and background, he'll understand your message much faster.

The top sales producers are *decorators of the commonplace.* They make even mundane things seem exciting and provocative.

Try this: During the next two days, whenever you explain something that might be even remotely difficult to understand, create a metaphor from your listener's viewpoint. See if it doesn't help you become more charismatic in his eyes. Or tell a story that explains how others have used your product or service with wonderful results. Find out if you can make that listener understand your ideas more quickly and fast-forward all your sales to successful conclusions.

CHAPTER 15

Breaking Rapport

Throughout this book, I discuss the importance of establishing and gaining rapport. But breaking rapport is also necessary from time to time. Has a salesperson ever approached you when you didn't have the time? You might have wanted him to leave, but you couldn't tell him so because you didn't want to be impolite. Or has a prospect ever become too talkative and gone off on a tangent while you were trying to sell something? He might have wanted to discuss politics or religion—and that can take up a lot of your valuable time. In either case, you probably found it difficult to say,

Let's go back to the subject at hand,

or

Hey, let's stay on track.

How and When to Break Rapport

You *can* break rapport with people without ever appearing rude. It's possible for you to break rapport without your prospect even realizing that you have terminated the conversation or redirected the topic.

Once, when I was speaking to a prospect about sales training, he started to discuss the problems he was having with his staff: His secretaries were demanding more money because they thought they were underpaid, and, as a result, he was having a very high turnover rate. He wanted to talk about getting more productivity from his secretaries despite the fact that they were underpaid. I wanted to talk about doing sales training for his sales group.

I realized we had come to cross-purposes. We could have been there for three hours without fulfilling my agenda for the meeting. So I decided to break rapport.

He and I were both sitting forward, talking about his staff. I sat back and went so far as to break eye contact. He kept talking, but at the same time he realized unconsciously that my interest was waning. He hesitated and paused, and I took that opportunity to redirect the conversation back to sales training. In this way, I kept the conversation on the track of my agenda.

That may sound a little abrasive or rude, but this man didn't sense anything of the kind. He only perceived that the conversation was being redirected and never consciously realized that I had broken rapport.

Mismatching

One of the most effective ways to break rapport is simply by mismatching body posture. Do not mirror. If the person crosses his legs, uncross yours. If he leans back, you sit forward. If he talks slowly, you talk fast.

I once dealt with a manager who knew exactly how to break rapport with telephone salespeople. During the conversation, he doesn't want to say, "I'm busy. Call me another time." Instead, he taps the receiver with a pencil while the salesperson talks. Obviously this distracts the telephone salesperson enough to unnerve him. That manager told me that this rapport-breaking technique was almost 100 percent effective.

Recognizing When Rapport Is Being Broken

Rapport breaks are often used by businesspeople to sabotage meetings. I've heard many stories about meetings between salespeople and business executives during which one or two of the executives would purposely mismatch and break rapport after it had been established. They didn't want to see the meeting culminate in a sale.

Have you ever been involved with two or more people in making your sale? Have you ever given a presentation to a few people whose agreement was needed to confirm the purchase of your product?

I was privy to such a meeting. Before the meeting started, I listened to what people were saying about a pension product that was about to be presented by a very sharp salesperson. The individual who was the salesperson's closest confidant had already bought into the concept. He was very confident and felt comfortable with the salesperson's easygoing manner as well as with the product's benefits.

But as I listened to the other people talking around the room, I found that another individual there wanted a different company to provide this service. A friend of his sold a similar product that wasn't even being considered by the company. Unfortunately, his attitude was that if his friend couldn't have the business, the company shouldn't give it to anybody.

At first, while the presentation was going on, this negative executive was fairly attentive, but after four or five minutes, I noticed that everybody around the table was leaning forward in a buying posture except for this one man.

He leaned back away from the table with his arms and legs crossed and avoided eye contact with the salesman practically the whole time. He was almost rude because of the disinterest he was showing.

Well, as you might have guessed, since a unanimous vote was needed, he sabotaged the meeting. When the other individuals around the table saw him breaking rapport, they in turn grew unsettled. The sale was lost.

I talked to a salesman recently who sells a financial product called keyman insurance. In one case, the decision maker had matched, mirrored, and maintained high rapport throughout the interview, but when it came time to close, he broke rapport, leaned back in his chair, and avoided eye contact. In counseling the prospect, the salesman found out that the decision maker was afraid of facing his own death and wanted to avoid discussing it, which is why the close was so difficult; closing was like the prospect's admitting his own mortality.

Teasing

Still other people will break rapport with you only because they subsconsciously want you to pursue them to try to reestablish it. One very interesting technique they may use is called *teasing*.

Young women and men match and mirror members of the opposite sex very closely. When a potential love interest crosses his or her legs, so does the person who is teasing. One leans forward when the other does. The teaser may even match voice tone, pace, and pitch. During a conversation, the teaser will even match the other's words.

Then suddenly, like lightning, the teaser breaks off all rapport, going so far as to avoid eye contact, crossing arms and legs, and leaving the person being teased feeling totally mystified, sincerely thinking he or she has done something wrong. So the teasee tries to regain rapport by leaning forward and paying more attention, acting as though he or she is pleading for his or her life.

In the suspense film *No Way Out*, the film's male lead is in full uniform at a presidential inaugural ball. Just prior to his arrival, we see his love interest ask a man to light her cigarette and then quickly break rapport. The star arrives on the scene, lights the woman's cigarette, and says, "You're very impressed with me." She denies it. "Yes, you are," he says, then walks away. He has established rapport quickly, then broken it by leaving. The next scene shows her following him.

By establishing and then breaking rapport, the dashing navy commander piques the woman's interest and causes her to try to regain rapport.

You too can use the technique of *breaking rapport* in your sales efforts. You will be amazed by the increase in your customers' commitment to you and your products.

CHAPTER 16

Buying Signals

Even if you've identified your prospect as a visual, auditory, or kinesthetic and then used every subliminal selling technique effectively, you won't make money unless you can close. Knowing *when* to close may make you more money than knowing *how*. This chapter identifies signals that will help you let your prospect buy when he's ready to buy instead of when you are.

A bright and articulate salesperson, Hiram, recently presented the perfect product to a qualified and interested prospect, Larry, who had been referred to him by a mutual friend. The referral was so strong that Hiram easily established rapport with Larry in his sales presentation.

During the probing phase of their conversation, Hiram discovered that Larry really needed his product. Hiram presented his product masterfully. He tailored each feature exactly to Larry's needs, matching his primary mode of communication throughout the process.

Hiram was really proud of the technical expertise he displayed during the presentation. Unfortunately, Hiram kept talking, talking, and talking until Larry looked anxiously at his watch. He cut short the interview, telling Hiram that he had another appointment scheduled.

What had gone wrong? Hiram was a great prober and presenter. He had matched Larry's primary mode of communication and had established what seemed to be great rapport.

There is, however, another stage to a sale after probing and presenting. Remember: *No money is made unless you can close.* No commissions will fall into your pocket unless you are able to read your prospect's *buying signals.*

Signals for When to Close

Up to 30 percent of all sales are lost because the salesperson doesn't know *when* to close. Every single aspect of your prospect's behavior can give you insights you can use to close a sale. The following information highlights some buying signals you can look out for. Recognizing buying signals will give you the ability to know when your prospect wants to buy.

Head-Nod and Smile

The most basic buying signal, which even beginners will recognize, is a smile with a "yes" head-nodding motion. Although this does not necessarily mean that a prospect will buy at that precise moment, it is an indication that the prospect is ready to buy, especially if his head-nod and smile are more pronounced than when he first entered the room.

The faster your prospect nods his head, the more he's thinking,

> I wish this salesperson would just shut up.

By nodding quickly, the prospect is indicating,

> I've heard this all before. Move on before I start to
> get bored.

At this moment you should ask the prospect,

> I sense that this is pretty familiar territory to you.
> Where have you heard it before?

Proud to display his knowledge, your prospect will clue you in on what he already knows. Listen carefully, because he also may give you some indication of the hot buttons that will cause him to buy.

Pupil Dilation

When a prospect is excited or enthusiastic, his pupils will expand. You might be thinking, "Kerry, I don't get close enough to my prospect to see his pupils."

You ought to. A majority of your prospects, no matter what the light level, will involuntarily display pupil dilation (a widening of the pupils of the eye) when they are highly enthusiastic about your ideas.

Have you ever played poker? If so, you may have noticed someone at the poker table wearing sunglasses to hide his excitement over a good hand.

Aristotle Onasis, the late Greek shipping tycoon, was rumored to always wear sunglasses during intense business negotiations. If he didn't have his sunglasses with him, he would postpone his business meeting until he found a pair. He, however, refused to negotiate a deal if the person he was negotiating with wore sunglasses.

Buyer's Possessiveness

One of the most sophisticated buying signals is your prospect showing ownership of handouts and illustrations. Do you give your prospect illustrations to look at during a presentation? Watch what he does with them afterward. He may glance over the sheet of paper and set it down, return it to your side of the conference table, or even push it away. If he does one of these, he is showing *psychological dispossessiveness*, and signalling to you,

> The idea is not very impressive. My trust in you is
> low. I don't buy it.

If you see this nonverbal cue, you may wish to go back to the probing stage. Find out his real needs and desires. Don't attempt to close yet.

On the other hand, he may look at an illustration for a few moments. Then he may lay the sheet on his side of the table or desk. He may even clutch it and ask, "Is this my copy?"

His message is obvious.

A clear example of buyer possessiveness that went undetected by an inexperienced salesperson occurred when I accompanied him on an appointment. During the presentation stage, the prospect was given a fact sheet. He immediately drew it closer to him. He was possessive of the sheet and kept it without asking for the copy. To my amazement, the salesperson continued the presentation for more than forty-five minutes. I saw the prospect go from moderate interest via his buying signals, to apathy. The salesperson, in the course of one hour, had his prospect ready to buy. But he failed to note an obvious buying signal and then saw his prospect back out of a sale.

If you don't close your prospect at the right time, you will buy your product right back from him.

Chin Rubbing

While prospects are evaluating products, most will show some nonverbal sign indicating they are in deep thought. One might scratch his head while another may tense his lips. The most overt of these buying decision signals is the chin-rub.

If your prospect exhibits this behavior, stop talking immediately. He is deciding whether or not to buy. If you keep talking, you will confuse and intimidate him. If you see the chin-rub, stop talking, simply wait for a few seconds, and then pull out your contract for the prospect to sign. Of course, he may give you an objection after he stops rubbing his chin. But you will be surprised by how many of your prospects will say yes at this point, and all because you knew when to stop talking.

Whistling Teapot and Sitting Tremor Positions

In the numerous hours of videotaped sales interviews I've studied, I've noted an intriguing relationship between the way a prospect sits and his level of interest in what the salesperson is trying to sell to him.

Most good salespeople understand that a prospect who sits back in his chair with his arms folded and legs crossed may not be very receptive. But when that same prospect moves forward or sits on the edge of his chair, he is in what I refer as the *whistling teapot position,* because he is just as ready to buy as a kettle of hot water is to be steeped into tea, and you've got the sale.

An even more dramatic buying position is the *sitting tremor signal.* It is also displayed by leaning forward or sitting on the edge of a chair. But in the sitting tremor position, the prospect has one hand on his knee and the other forearm on his thigh. These people are enthusiastic to buy.

Tom O'Neil, a top-producing salesperson in Lansing, Michigan, almost missed one of the biggest sales of his career. His prospect, a successful business owner, seemed to be giving buying signals. Tom had determined his prospect's needs the first day and the second day presented his product. After an hour into the presentation, the owner moved into the sitting tremor position. Tom remembered my advice to him on buying signals and decided to stop talking. Tom pulled the sales agreement out and used a simple assumptive close. His prospect signed immediately and smiled. Tom took him out to dinner that night and asked him why he had said yes so quickly. The prospect replied that he had been ready to buy thirty minutes before Tom had stopped talking and that Tom had actually been talking him out of the sale. Tom had been in the process of buying his product back from the prospect!

Million-dollar sales producers know that knowing when to close is as important as how to close. If you watch for your prospect's buying signals, you will close at least 30 percent more prospects.

CHAPTER 17

Putting It All Together

If your behavioral tool chest consists only of a hammer, you'll tend to treat everything like a nail.

But all of your prospects are different. You learned about neuro-linguistic programming in Chapters 1 through 4 and how to recognize and sell to your visual, auditory, and kinesthetic prospects. Chapters 5 through 15 discussed the importance of building rapport, techniques you can use to maintain rapport, how to turn it into a sale, and how to break it when necessary. In Chapter 16, you learned that you should sell to your prospect by recognizing when he is ready to buy. This chapter shows you how to integrate all of the ideas you've gained throughout this book so that you will say the right thing to the right person at the right time and build a successful selling career.

What follows is a close account of a meeting between a first-time prospect and a financial services salesperson who has become an expert in the use of subliminal selling skills. You'll get a chance not only to read the dialogue between Dennis, the salesperson, and Chuck, the prospect, but to avail yourself of an analysis directly afterward. Try to remember what you've learned, and do your own play-by-play as you read the dialogue.

The Sales Dialogue

DENNIS: Hi, Chuck.

CHUCK: Hi.

DENNIS: It was nice of Jim Lewis to refer me to you. Have you known Jim long?

CHUCK: Yeah, for a couple of years. We play tennis together.

DENNIS: Oh, that's great. I play tennis too. I think without it I'd suffer from dunlap disease. That's where your stomach done lapped over your belt.

CHUCK [*laughing*]:   Yeah, I know what you mean.

DENNIS: Chuck, as I mentioned to you on the telephone, I'm a financial planner. Tell me, what does financial planning mean to you?

CHUCK: Well, in my view, I see financial planning as a way to protect yourself from abusive taxes and help plan for future needs. Right?

DENNIS: Right. You seem surprisingly informed already. It's important for me to know what you think about financial planning to give us a place to start out. You obviously are fairly familiar with personal economics already. One more question: Chuck, what do you see yourself accomplishing as a result of our meeting today?

CHUCK: Well, I envision finding out more about my financial weaknesses and some of the mistakes I've made. But I also want to buy a new house in the next year. I'd like to cover some ways that I can use my money better in making purchases like that.

DENNIS: Why do you picture yourself buying a new house?

CHUCK: Well, I like the one I'm in. But some friends have said that buying a rental property may be a smart move. What do you think?

DENNIS: Well, if you don't mind tying up a lot of money for a few years and are willing to spend a lot of time managing the property, it could be pretty lucrative. But let's assume it's five years down the road. What has happened to let you know that an investment like this has been good for you?

CHUCK: That's a tough question. I guess the property has appreciated 15 to 20 percent every year, I've only spent a few hours a month with property maintenance, and I've been able to write off most of it on my income taxes.

DENNIS: So, 15 to 20 percent appreciation, a few hours maintenance, and income tax writeoffs are important to you. Correct?

CHUCK: Yeah, I guess.

DENNIS: I had a client come in here last week who had much the same picture of his objectives as you. We first met five years ago, just as you and I are meeting today. He was a teacher, just like you. Now, five years later he's off sailing for six months in the Caribbean with his wife and son. The interesting thing is that five years ago he had about as much money as you have now but received 28 percent on his invested dollars. He hasn't had to spend even one hour maintaining a rental property. Are you interested in how he did it?

CHUCK: You bet.

DENNIS: He put his money into what is called a real estate limited partnership.

CHUCK: Now wait a second. I've looked at those before. You stick a pile of money in and the IRS may just come along and say, "We don't like this one; it's too abusive." If the company I invested in went bust, then I'd be stuck. At least with my own rental house, I could write off the losses and improvements.

DENNIS: I understand why you think that way. Have you heard about due diligence?

CHUCK: No.

DENNIS: This is where an army of attorneys and CPAs in my company check out every nook and cranny of the partnership to make sure that whatever the real estate company promises, they deliver on. This is all done to protect you, Chuck. What's your feeling on this?

CHUCK: Due diligence, huh?

DENNIS: Is this IRS thing the only part that is of concern to you?

CHUCK: Yes, but I guess not anymore. But will you guarantee that this due diligence will forestall any problems?

DENNIS: Can't do that, Chuck. But let's look at this color chart showing the track record of this partnership for the last fifteen years. You can see here where it has averaged 30 percent for seven years straight.

CHUCK: Yeah, wow, that's a lot better than rental property for that time period.

DENNIS: One more thing, Chuck. The family sailing in the Caribbean—the reason why they did so well is that they bought into the partnership quickly, Chuck. If you don't mind, I'm going to call in my secretary with the agreement forms so we can take advantage of this investment. By the way, we should meet again. How's next Monday at 3 or Tuesday at 4?

CHUCK: I like your style. This track record shows that it's exactly what I need. Let's meet again on Tuesday. And I'll be right back. I have to go out to my car to get my checkbook.

The Play-by-Play

How many subliminal selling skills did you notice Dennis using? Let's go over them together.

1. Dennis immediately established rapport by talking about Jim Lewis.
2. He also used humor to relax Chuck.
3. Dennis then asked Chuck what financial planning meant to him so he could find out Chuck's thought mode. Chuck is a visual. Remember, he said, "my view is."
4. Dennis complimented Chuck, by saying, "You seem surprisingly well informed." This was to establish higher rapport.
5. Dennis tried to find Chuck's outcomes for the meeting by asking what he wanted to accomplish. Did you hear Dennis match Chuck's visual mode by asking, "What do you *see* yourself accomplishing?"
6. Dennis wanted more information about Chuck's outcomes than just his desire to buy a rental property, so he used the let's-assume fantasy technique: "Let's assume it's five years down the road." By using this technique, Dennis found the three key decision points that were motivating Chuck to find a rental house.
7. Dennis actively listened and played back these three points as a check on what he had just heard. This also increased trust and showed Chuck that Dennis cared.
8. Dennis then used a metaphor and a story to get Chuck to identify himself with a successful investor who was sailing carefree in the Caribbean. Dennis used this story to get Chuck to consider a real estate limited partnership.
9. Chuck promptly produced an objection, so Dennis slid into the auditory mode, by asking: "Have you heard about due diligence?" He then used a most important point in cashing objections: He asked Chuck if he had any other concerns before he continued. This prevented an objection duel that could have lasted a long time.
10. Chuck was then shown a color graph of the partnership's track record, which Chuck loved because of his need for information he could see to comprehend data better. Remember, Chuck was a visual.
11. Trying to close Chuck, Dennis gave a hidden command. He mentioned that the family sailing in the Caribbean bought into the partnership quickly. Dennis did an assumptive close, rescheduled another appointment with an alternative choice close by saying, "We'll meet again Monday at 3 or Tuesday at 4," and made the sale.

The purpose of these techniques is to *help* your clients buy what they want and need, not to manipulate them into buying for your own good. If these techniques are used with a selfish purpose, you may win a few, but the word will get around and you will lose far more than you will ever win. Used correctly, you will produce more business than ever before.

Practice, Practice, Practice

You've learned a lot of new ideas in this book. They are simple and effective. They also represent some of the newest techniques in sales psychology.

You will find that the more you actively practice these skills in your day-to-day business, the sooner they'll become a natural part of your sales efforts. Even the time you spent reading this book has enabled you to assimilate much of the information that will help you get through to your clients and prospects as never before.

Let's recap and summarize the ideas you've learned—the subliminal selling skills:

• *First*, you learned about the behavior of charismatic people—what makes some people so successful. You learned how people think, how your prospects relate to you, and how you can get through to them. You know that there are three modes people fit into: visual, auditory, and kinesthetic. You found out that each type wants to be dealt with in his own particular way.

• *Second*, you learned in depth about visuals. You saw that visuals' minds work like a photo album full of snapshots. They look up to the right, up to the left, or straight ahead while you speak to them. These visuals use words such as:

show	*view*
bright	*see*
clear	

You found out that visuals want to see your ideas. They want you to show them a lot of illustrations. They can understand your message more quickly by trying to visualize it.

• *Third*, you learned about auditories. You heard that their mind works like a jukebox, the arm picking the record out, putting it on a platter, and then playing it to understand what you're talking about. These auditories want to hear your message delivered well. They get a lot out of sounds. They use words such as:

bear   *sounds*
rings   *tell*

Auditories want you to match their predicates and use the words of the mode they think in.

You learned that they listen to the inflection of your voice. They want you to use clever sayings. They want soft background music. They want you to verbally explain illustrations; they don't want to read them.

• *Fourth,* you learned about kinesthetics. These individuals feel good or bad about you very quickly. These are the people who use words such as:

feel   *touch*
impression   *grab*

They want you to communicate with them using these same words.

Kinesthetics want you to give them things they can hold. They want to become involved in the conversation. They want to experience it by holding, touching, and feeling.

• *Fifth,* you learned some highly useful techniques to gain rapport: how to use active listening to generate trust and warmth much more quickly, and how to match key words or the words people put great importance on during communication. These words reflect a frame of reference or the experience level of your prospect. They are also accompanied by phrases. You learned to match these words and phrases to try to get your prospects to better understand your message.

You gained information about voice quality, the pace, the pitch, the timbre, and the tone. When you match or mirror correctly, it creates higher comfort levels in your prospect. You learned how to mirror body movements and increase trust by using your hands, legs, and even your posture and also about cross-mirroring.

You learned techniques for breaking rapport when necessary—with no one noticing a thing. If there's a person you don't want to talk to or if a meeting starts to go off on a tangent away from your goals, you can break rapport and try to get back on track.

In the chapter on anchoring, you learned about changing your and your prospect's emotions. You should now realize that there are unique ways to answer visually, auditorially, and kinesthetically by doing things like raising your eyebrows for the visuals, makings sounds and noises for the auditories, and touching for the kinesthetics. You also discovered how to steal anchors: getting your prospect to understand you five times as fast by using the same nonverbal symbols he uses on others.

You learned about how to get your prospect to be more open, honest, and accepting of you and how to keep him from feeling stuck in an objection by taking him from one thought mode to another. You know that if he's stuck on price, you can move him into another benefit unrelated to price. You know that when an objection exists in one thought mode, it may not exist in another.

You also know how to use hidden commands, commands that you can imbed in your own stories to get your prospect to act on your message. You learned steps to cash objections, get outcomes, find out what your prospect really wants so you can give it to him, and then dovetail his needs and outcomes with your own.

You know that you can involve your prospect in what you're saying by using metaphors and stories that tie in loosely to your prospect's own experience or situation.

You learned how to make your prospect see, feel, and hear himself in the situation by getting him to experience it through your stories and metaphors.

You learned to let your prospect buy when he is ready to buy, not when you are ready to have him buy. You discovered some buying signals that are easily recognizable in prospects.

All of these techniques can literally change the way you sell, even though much of this information relies on common sense, since these are things people tend to do naturally. *But if you can turn them into your tools instead of haphazard accidents, you will sell more than ever before.*

Take common sense and make it common practice.

By remembering these subliminal sales skills, you'll possess more useful information than many other salespeople. You will gain strength and have the ability to communicate with people in exactly the way they want.

Recently I wrote an article for a sales magazine. One month later I received the following letter from a man in central Pennsylvania:

> Dear Kerry:
>
> I have been using what I had thought were
> extremely good standard sales techniques for about five
> years. My business was doing well, but not great.
> Kerry, I used some of the techniques outlined in your
> article about the visuals, auditories, and
> kinesthetics, finding outcomes, anchoring, as well as
> instant replay.
>
> I wouldn't have thought it was possible so
> quickly, but I have received three more sales this week
> alone that I don't think would have happened if I
> hadn't used this information.

Remember, it's up to you now to make these ideas useful. Don't try to apply them all at once—just a couple of new techniques every day. Reread parts of this book and you'll get something new each time. Apply subliminal selling skills, and you will increase your business by more than 50 percent.

In your business, knowledge is power, power is flexibility, and flexibility is having all the options you need to make all the right moves at the right time.

Glossary

active listening   The process of actively listening to the prospect so that he knows you are interested in his needs and wants. It consists of valuing the speaker, developing the desire to hear the truth, making sure you don't interrupt your prospect, listening intensely, and trying to understand from your prospect's point of view by showing respect for his comments, maintaining good eye contact, and avoiding clichés that will generate only superficial rapport.

anchoring   The technique of eliciting people's memories and emotions by using verbal or nonverbal cues. By anchoring, you can subliminally change a prospect's attitude. The best time to create an anchor is when rapport is at its peak. You can use a touch, a smile, a point of a finger, a raise of your eyebrows, or a snap of your fingers to create an associate with a moment of trust. You will be able to recall that trust or high rapport instantly by using the same gesture you used when rapport first was established.

auditories   Prospects who buy not because of what they see or feel but because of how you talk about your products or ideas. They listen more closely to *how* you say something than to what you actually say. Auditories make up approximately 25 percent of your prospect base.

auditory predicates   Those words that are particularly appealing to auditories, such as "tone," "static," "hear," "ring," "sound," "say," and "tell."

behavioral cues   Behavior patterns that indicate how a prospect will react in a sales situation.

buyer possessiveness   Your prospect's indication of ownership of handouts and illustrations, one of the most sophisticated of the buying signals. He may look at an illustration for a few moments, then lay it on his side of the table or desk. He may even clutch it and ask, "Is this my copy?"

buying signals   The aspects of a prospect's behavior that provide you with information for closing in a sale. Recognizing buying signals lets you know when your prospect wants to buy. Some buying signals to look out for are the head nod and smile, pupil dilation, buyer possessiveness, psychological dispossessiveness, chin rubbing, the whistling teapot position, and the sitting tremor signal.

calibration   The act of noticing what your prospect looks like when he's interested in what you are saying—determining his unique set of nonverbal cues so that you know what he is thinking. For example, if you notice that when he's interested and happy, he leans forward, when he leans back, he may be showing you negativity or even defensiveness.

cashing objections   A method of turning an objection into an acceptance. Three steps in cashing an objection are acknowledging the objection, uncovering the intent behind it, and resolving it subliminally.

chin rubbing   A buying signal. While prospects are evaluating products, most will display some nonverbal sign indicating that they are in deep thought. One might scratch his head, while another may tense his lips. The most overt of these buying decision signals is the chin rub. If your prospect exhibits such behavior, stop talking immediately! He is deciding whether or not to buy. If you keep talking, you will confuse and intimidate him.

choral unison   Typically, a mirroring of not only body language but voice, pace, and speed. People in unison are actually trying to be more like each other in an effort to decrease their verbal, physical, and behavioral differences.

crossover mirroring   Imitating one nonverbal gesture with a different part of the body. For example, if your prospect crosses his arms, you cross your legs. If your prospect rests his head on his hand, you may touch your chin. If your prospect's hands are in his pockets, you fold your hands in your lap very close to your pockets.

diffusion or disassociation   A method of getting away from an objection or negative reaction when you try to close a sale too quickly. By disassociating yourself from the objection, you can close later on in the sales presentation.

dovetailing outcomes   Letting your prospect know your outcomes and showing him that you will do your best to help him to reach his outcomes.

feel, felt, found technique   Used to try to counter a prospect's objections, in which you say something to the effect of: "I understand how you *feel*. Other prospects have *felt* the same way until they *found* out that. . . ." Substitute "feel" and "felt" with "see" and "view" for visuals and "hear" and "told" for auditories.

head-nod and smile   The most basic of buying signals, a "yes" head-nodding motion. Although this does not necessarily mean that a prospect will buy at that precise moment, it is an indication that the prospect is ready to buy, especially if his head-nod and smile are more pronounced than when he first entered the room.

hidden commands or trigger words   Certain phrases that generate specific responses. These phrases tend to get prospects to think the way you'd like them to think. The concept of giving hidden commands revolves around underlining certain parts of your ideas to help the prospect focus on certain product benefits or ideas to which you think they will respond. Using phrases like, "Evan, this will work for you," is effective if "work for you" is emphasized. Another effective technique is to make a hidden command out of your prospect's favorite phrase.

instant replay technique   Finding out why your prospect bought a particular product in the past and "replaying" those reasons for him so that he will buy again. You assume that he will buy in the future in a fashion similar to the way he bought in the past. You take the information he gives you and play it back to him.

kinesthetic predicates   Those words are phrases that are particularly appealing to kinesthetics, such as "touch base," "handle," "grab," "rub," and "feel."

kinesthetics   Prospects who buy because of a visceral ("gut") feeling. They establish trust as a result of the way they feel about you, have deep emotions about you, feel hot or cold about you very quickly, like or dislike you very fast, and get goose bumps often. They make up approximately 40 percent of your prospect base.

leading   Used to lead a client to behavior or reactions you desire. Unlike pacing, leading comes after you have established rapport. Once you've established rapport with your prospects, you have the power to move them in the direction you want them to go. On the physical level, chances are your prospect will move his body or posture in the same way you do. But as you are leading them with your body, you can also get them to begin accepting your goals.

"let's assume" fantasy technique   A useful tool to help you get your prospect to tell you what he likes best about your product, even though he has never bought a product like yours before. A let's-assume fantasy tries to project your prospect into the future with your product by forcing him to think one hour, one month, or ten years ahead—to imagine what he liked about the product and how it helped him.

life events and social readjustment rating scale   A scale developed by Thomas Holmes to show how stressful change in our lives can be.

marking out   Pausing just before and after using selective, often highly important words.

matching or mirroring   Matching the prospect's key words, phrases, and actions.

mental map   A prospect's unique way of thinking. When you begin to understand your prospect's mental map, you will know how to communicate the right messages to him. He will grasp what you are saying, as well as the intent behind your words, and communicate it back to you.

metaphor   A figure of speech or a verbal association that generates emotion in the listener. Any verbal association or story that helps your prospect identify or see himself as part of your ideas will enable him to understand your ideas much faster.

mismatching   The opposite of mirroring or matching a prospect. If a prospect crosses his legs, you uncross yours. If he leans back, you sit forward. If he talks slowly, you talk fast. If you want to establish rapport, never mismatch a prospect; but if you are trying to break it, mismatching is very effective.

neuro-linguistic programming (NLP)   The theory that your prospects fit into three basic groups: visuals, kinesthetics, and auditories, based on the research of Richard Bandler and John Grinder, two psychology researchers at the University of Santa Cruz. Bandler and Grinder wanted to uncover the ways people think so that psychotherapists could resolve psychological problems more effectively by looking at how patients and clients used language and at the thought process behind that language.

nonverbal matching or mirroring   A nonverbal method of establishing rapport by matching a person's physical actions.

outcomes   Not only your prospect's needs and desires but also his perception of what he wants. When your prospect talks to you about buying your product, he's only trying to see, hear, or feel himself with your product in the future. He's trying to imagine a possible outcome of using your product.

pace   The speed of your voice.

pacing   Moving all of your behavioral makeup to fit your prospect—whether it's voice mode, nonverbal cues, or phrases. When you pace a prospect, you are trying to be as close to your prospect mentally as possible.

pitch   How high or low your voice is.

psychological dispossessiveness   A negative buying signal, where the prospect does not take possession of the material you hand him. He may glance over the sheet of paper and set it down. He may return it to your side of the conference table or even push it away. If you see this nonverbal cue, you may wish to go back to the probing stage.

psychological sliding   A way to move your prospect from his objections in one mode of communication (visual, auditory, or kinesthetic) to realizing the benefits of the product in another mode.

pupil dilation   Expansion of pupils when a prospect is excited or enthusiastic. A majority of prospects' pupils dilate involuntarily when they are highly enthusiastic about an idea.

rapport   A sympathetic and harmonious relationship between you and your prospect. Rapport helps the person you're communicating with find meaning and intent in what you say. It also helps him to feel comfortable with you and creates a feeling of warmth and understanding. In selling, rapport makes prospects feel that what you're saying is aimed directly at them and at their particular needs and desires. A high rapport relationship is marked by harmony, conformity, accord, or affinity.

reframing   An act of changing the words that traditionally label a concept or idea. For example, by simply asking, "How is your day going?" you force your prospect to really think about their day. "How are you?" basically asks the same thing, but your prospect's automatic trigger response to the question causes him to reply with "fine" without even thinking about your question.

romantic dance   Often seen in husbands and wives or couples whose rapport is high. They sit, walk, and stand alike, and also change positions in sync with one another.

self-talk   A process through which people actually talk out events to themselves to solve problems more quickly and effectively.

sitting tremor signal   A buying signal in which the prospect leans forward or sits on the edge of his chair with one hand on his knee and the other forearm on his thigh. This person is ready to buy.

stealing anchors   Using your prospect's own exclusive nonverbal communication methods and techniques. If you steal someone's personal anchors, you can use them to establish rapport instead of having to create new ones.

subliminal selling skills   Techniques that enable you to sell to your prospect subconsciously by identifying and communicating in his thought mode so that he buys products and services from you. Subliminal selling skills help identify a prospect's buying patterns so that you can fill his needs.

timbre   The resonance of your voice.

tonal auditories   People who make sense of what you are talking about by vocalizing to themselves and having internal conversations. When a tonal auditory looks down and to the left, he is actually thinking about what you are saying to him by trying to compare what you are talking about to what he has heard before. He may be comparing your ideas to what he thinks he should be hearing.

unconscious competence   A trait of successful salespeople who can't tell you *how* they are selling but are successful nonetheless.

visual predicates   Those words that are particularly appealing to the visual, such as "show," "clear," "bright," "picture," and "see."

visuals   Those individuals who understand more from what they see than from what they hear or feel. Visuals make up approximately 35 percent of your prospect base.

whistling teapot position   A buying signal where the prospect sits forward or sits on the edge of his chair, indicating that he is ready to buy.

Suggested Reading

Books

Bandler, Richard, and John Grinder. *Frogs Into Princes: Neuro-Linguistic Programming.* Moab, Utah: Real People Press, 1979.

Boyan, Lee. *Successful Cold Call Selling.* New York: AMACOM, 1985.

Brill, A. A., ed. *The Basic Writings of Sigmund Freud.* New York: Modern Library, 1938.

Buzzotta, V. R., et. al. *Effective Selling Through Psychology: Dimensional Sales and Sales Management Strategies.* Cambridge, Mass.: Ballinger, 1982.

Campbell, Sarah F., ed. *Piaget Sampler: An Introduction to Piaget Through His Own Words.* Ann Arbor, Mich.: Books on Demand/University Microfilms International, 1976.

Delmar, Ken. *Winning Moves: The Body Language of Selling.* New York: Warner, 1985.

Evered, James F. *A Motivational Approach to Selling.* New York: AMACOM, 1982.

Fenton, Lois, with Edward Olcott. *Dress for Excellence.* New York: Rawson Associates, 1986.

Freud, Sigmund. *On Creativity and the Unconscious*, reprinted. New York: Harper, 1958.

Johnson, Kerry L. *Peak Performance Selling: How to Increase Your Sales by 70% Within 6 Weeks.* Englewood Cliffs, N.J.: Prentice-Hall, 1988.

——. *Mastering the Game: The Human Edge in Sales and Marketing.* Tustin, Cal.: Louis and Ford, 1987

Key, Wilson Bryan. *Subliminal Seduction.* New York: New American Library, 1973.

Ostrander, Sheila, and Lynn Schroeder. *Superlearning.* New York: Dell, 1982.

Piaget, Jean. *The Grasp of Consciousness: Action and Concept in the Young Child,* reprinted. Cambridge, Mass.: Harvard University Press, 1976.

——. *The Mechanisms of Perception.* London: Routledge & Kegan Paul, 1969.

Savage, John. *High Touch Selling.* Chicago: Longman, 1986.

——. *It's Getting Easier.* Cincinnati: National Underwriter, 1980.

Schock, Kenneth. *Psychology of Successful Selling.* Dubuque, Ia.: Kendall/Hunt, 1986.

Seglin, Jeffrey L. *Marketing Financial Advisory Services: A Hands-On Guide.* Englewood Cliffs, N.J.: Prentice-Hall, 1988.

Sheehan, Don, and John O'Toole. *Shut Up and Sell: Tested Techniques for Closing the Sale.* New York: AMACOM, 1984.

Singer, Dorothy G., and Tracey A. Revenson. *A Piaget Primer: How a Child Thinks.* New York: New American Library, 1978.

Skinner, B. F. *About Behaviorism.* New York: Random House, 1976.

——. *Beyond Freedom and Dignity.* New York: Bantam, 1972.

Audio and Video

Johnson, Kerry L. *How to Read Your Client's Mind* (audiocassette tapes). International Productivity Systems, Inc., Box 1404, Tustin, Cal. 92681.

——. *How To Read Your Client's Mind* (video). International Productivity Systems, Inc., Box 1404, Tustin, Cal. 92681.

——. *The Psychology of Productivity* (audiocassette tapes). International Productivity Systems, Inc., Box 1404, Tustin, Cal. 92681.

——. *Solving The People Puzzle* (audiocassette tapes). International Productivity Systems, Inc., Box 1404, Tustin, Cal. 92681.

——. *Stress Survival* (audiocassette tapes). International Productivity Systems, Inc., Box 1404, Tustin, Cal. 92681.

——. *Tele-Sales: How to Get Business on the Telephone* (audiocassette tapes). International Productivity Systems, Inc., Box 1404, Tustin, Cal. 92681.

Waitley, Denis. *The Inner Winner* (audiocassette tapes). Chicago: Nightingale-Conant.

Walther, George. *Profitable Telemarketing.* (audiocassette tapes). Chicago: Nightingale-Conant.

Ziglar, Zig. *Sell Your Way to the Top.* (audiocassette tapes). Chicago: Nightingale-Conant.

Periodicals

Abbott, William, "Buyer Confidence on the Seller." *Folio: The Magazine for Magazine Management,* February 1985, pp. 107 ff.

Bower, Bruce, "Subliminal Messages: Changes for the Better?" *Science News,* March 8, 1986, pp. 156 ff.

Carter, Roy, "Whispering Soft Nothings to Stop the Thief: How 'Reinforcement Messaging' Works." *Retail and Distribution Management,* January-February 1986, pp. 36 ff.

Caudill, Donald, "Color Management: A Nonverbal Communication Tool." *Journal of Systems Management.* January 1986, pp. 37 ff.

Cialdini, Robert, "The Triggers of Influence." *Psychology Today,* February 1984, pp. 43–44.

Costigan, Kelly, "How Color Goes to Your Head." *Science Digest,* December 1984, pp. 24 ff.

Dreyfack, Raymond, "The Selling Edge." *American Salesman,* December 1986, pp. 9 ff.

Egge, Eric, "Selling Power." *American Salesman,* December 1986, pp. 3 ff.

Gable, Myron, et al, "An Evaluation of Subliminally Embedded Sexual Stimuli in Graphics." *Journal of Advertising,* Winter 1987, pp. 26 ff.

Gilbert, Mark G., " 'He's Driving Me Crazy!'." *American Salesman,* September 1985, pp. 27 ff.

Haberstroh, Jack, "Can't Ignore Subliminal Ad Charges: Adfolk Laugh, But Students Listen." *Advertising Age,* September 17, 1984, pp. 3 ff.

Hall, Elizabeth, "Mining New Gold From Old Research: He Reworks Past Discoveries Looking for Basic Behavioral Processes That Are as Fundamental as Biological Processes." *Psychology Today,* February 1986, pp. 46 ff.

Johnson, Kerry L., "Dealing With the Fear of Success." *Manager's Magazine,* January 1986, pp. 24 ff.

——, "Influencing People With Color." *Financial Strategies,* Summer 1987, pp. 37 ff.

——, *The Sales Psychologist* (newsletter published quarterly). International Productivity Systems, Inc., Box 1404, Tustin, Cal. 92681.

Krugman, Herbert E., "Low Recall and High Recognition of Advertising." *Journal of Advertising Research,* February-March 1986, pp. 79 ff.

McLaughlin, Mark, "Subliminal Tapes Urge Shoppers to Heed The Warning Sounds of Silence: 'Don't Steal.' " *New England Business,* February 2, 1987, pp. 36 ff.

Piersen, William S., "Fine Tuning." *American Salesman*, December 1986, pp. 16 ff.

Piontek, Stephen, "Johnson Zeros In on Ways That Clients Think." *National Underwriter*, October 12, 1985, pp. 18 ff.

Robinson, Irwin, "Private Thoughts in Clients' Minds." *Travel Weekly*, August 30, 1984, pp. 1 ff.

Ross, Melvin H., "Getting Below Awareness." *Advertising Age*, December 17, 1984, pp. 16 ff.

——, "Scrutinizing Subliminal Ads." *Advertising Age.*, December 17, 1984, pp. 16 ff.

Seglin, Jeffrey L., "The Eyes Tell All." *Financial Planning*, August 1986, pp. 156 ff.

"Subliminal Messages; Subtle Crime Stoppers: Despite a Dubious Reputation, They're Used in More Than 1,000 Stores." *Chain Store Age*, July 1986, pp. 85 ff.

Thompson, David W., " 'Reading' Customer Behavior." *Bank Marketing*, November 1985, pp. 45 ff.

Tysee, Maryon, "What's Wrong With Blue Potatoes?" *Psychology Today*, December 1985, pp. 6 ff.

Wilkinson, Roderick, "Get the Best Out of Brainstorming." *American Salesman*, December 1986, pp. 21 ff.

Index